On Your 1
Thamessiut

The Upper Thames to Maidenhead

Ellen Lee and John Broughton

COUNTRYSIDE BOOKS
NEWBURY, BERKSHIRE

First published 2000
© Ellen Lee and John Broughton 2000

COUNTRYSIDE BOOKS
3 Catherine Road
Newbury, Berkshire

To view our complete range of books,
please visit us at
www.countrysidebooks.co.uk

ISBN 1 85306 628 1

Designed by Graham Whiteman

Photographs by Ellen Lee
Maps by Gelder design & mapping
Front cover picture supplied by
Cyclographic Publications

Produced through MRM Associates Ltd., Reading
Printed in Singapore

CONTENTS

AREA MAP SHOWING THE LOCATIONS OF THE RIDES

INTRODUCTION

Cycling is much more than a way of getting from A to B. Journeying by car, bus or train you exist in a state of limbo, places rushing past too fast to experience them and only start and destination having any solid reality. By bicycle, travelling becomes a complete sensory experience. You see, hear, smell and sometimes even touch your environment. You travel slowly enough to interact with your surroundings, to wave a greeting, to exchange a smile and to notice those small details which help define each place as unique. Yet you travel quickly enough to see the subtle changes in land use, architecture, contours and so on which mark out one area distinct from the next.

The rides in this book are all linked through their proximity to the River Thames. For at least 200,000 years, and more particularly throughout the last 6,000 years, the river has been a magnet to human settlement. From Neolithic man to the aristocrats of the 18th and the rich industrialists of the 20th century, all have been drawn to the river and have left their imprint on its countryside. The result is that, today, the Thames Valley offers some of the most pleasant and interesting rural countryside that you could wish to cycle in.

The routes vary in distance from 8 to 30 miles and even with visits to places of interest and stops for refreshment none should take more than five hours to complete. Generally the rides along the Upper Thames, between Kemble and Wallingford, are flat or gently undulating and are therefore recommended for beginners to cycling. To the east of the Goring Gap the routes are hillier as they explore the hills either side of the river. No hill is too steep though when climbed (or walked up) at your own pace, and these rides offer spectacular views.

Cycling is what you want it to be. Whether you like to ride on your own or with friends or family and whether you enjoy riding fast, savouring the physical pleasures of riding or whether you prefer to potter around in a more leisurely fashion, stopping en route to investigate nooks and crannies and savour the sights, sounds and tastes of the country . . . whatever and however you do it, we hope that this book and its suggested routes inspire you with a taste for bicycle adventures.

Ellen Lee and John Broughton

GUIDE TO USING THIS BOOK

Each route is preceded by information to help you:

The **number of miles** is the total for the ride. Apart from short distances on tracks and a couple of routes with towpath sections, all the rides are on roads with hard surfaces.

The brief **introduction** to the ride gives a broad picture of where the route goes and also mentions particular features that you will see.

The **maps** listed at the beginning of each ride are all Ordnance Survey maps and it is advisable to take them with you as the sketch maps give limited information.

The **starting point** includes a suggested car park where you can leave your vehicle whilst on the ride.

Places for refreshment, sometimes particular pubs or tearooms, are mentioned in the pre-ride information and others are just waiting for you to discover them. Don't forget Paragraph 211 of the Highway Code: You MUST NOT ride under the influence of drink or drugs.

THE ROUTES

It is a good idea to read right through a route before setting out so that you note any places where you want to spend more time. The routes have been arranged according to their position along the Thames rather than their length or difficulty, so just choose ones you like the look of.

The directions have been written as clearly as possible. Instructions to turn left or right are printed in bold, like this: **Turn L** at the T-junction; **bear R** when the road forks by the church. Instructions to continue straight over a crossroads or carry straight on are not in bold.

The directions include some description about the route, but at the end of each route there is more information about **places of interest**. These include notes about architecture, history, legends and people connected with each entry.

The map of the area on page 4 shows where the twenty routes are situated. Each route is accompanied by a simple **sketch map**. These maps are intended to give you a general idea of where the routes go but are not detailed enough to be route guides. The relevant OS Landranger Series map is always recommended.

BEFORE YOU START

This section is aimed at cyclists who have not ventured out on a touring ride before. It is important to go prepared so that if a problem occurs you are in a good position to cope with it. We have put together a few pointers to help you.

Firstly, make sure that your bicycle is in a roadworthy condition. Check the tyres for wear, or damage, and make sure that they are properly inflated. Check the brakes. Change badly worn blocks. Treat your bicycle as a friend and it will reward you with many miles of happy cycling.

Having made sure that your bicycle is well looked after, it is time to attend to your needs. Make sure that your bicycle is adjusted to suit you, as a wrongly adjusted machine can be very tiring and uncomfortable. If cycling alone the confidence and knowledge of how to deal with a puncture will bring peace of mind.

Always cycle in comfortable clothing, and go prepared with some waterproof outer wear, even if you think you won't need it. If cycling in the winter take an extra layer of warm clothing as well, just in case the temperature drops unexpectedly. It is a good idea to carry a drink (water will do) and a snack to fend off thirst and hunger. Water bottle carriers can be fitted to any bicycle.

Other things to carry with you should include a basic toolkit, puncture outfit, tyre levers and a spare inner tube, not forgetting a suitable pump. Most experienced cyclists change the inner tube if they have a puncture as it is easier than mending the puncture on the road.

Tip: Make sure that your toolkit contains a pair of long nosed pliers which are very useful for pulling out thorns etc when they have caused a puncture.

It is advisable to carry some money and identification, in case of emergency. Having taken these precautions you should be able to enjoy your cycle touring rides to the full, and with peace of mind.

All of these pointers are based upon experience gained from many thousands of cycling miles.

SAFETY

In general when cycling on a public highway obey the highway code, and use common sense. The wearing of helmets is not compulsory in the UK and is left to the discretion of the rider. It is a good idea to wear something light in colour so that other road users can see you. Remember that it is the responsibility of the cyclist to make himself, or herself, visible, especially in low light.

1

The Stripling Thames

27 miles

It is always satisfying to know how something starts, and this ride explores the beginnings of the River Thames, from its source to Cricklade, the first town on its banks. Several places claim to be the source of the Thames. We visit the currently favoured holder of the title, Thameshead, and then continue to Ewen. Here, you may be forgiven for not realising that the small stream which meanders around the outskirts of this picturesque village is the same river that is raced on by the students of Oxford or that flows majestically under the Regency bridge at Marlow. Humble beginnings certainly. We continue through the Cotswold Water Park, now a popular venue for wildlife and watersports. At its furthest point the ride enters the Saxon town of Cricklade, the only Thamesside town in Wiltshire, before returning to Kemble.

Map: OS Landranger 163 Cheltenham and Cirencester (GR 985974).

Starting point: This ride starts from Kemble railway station (on the line from Swindon to Gloucester and Cheltenham). By car, Kemble is located on the A429, 4 miles south-west of Cirencester. The station has an adjacent car park with a daily charge.

There are plenty of pubs along the route, and the Keynes Country Park has a lakeside café. Cricklade, the natural halfway point, has so many cafés, restaurants and pubs on its main street that it would be impossible to go hungry there! There is also a pub, the Tavern, which serves food next to the Kemble railway station.

The countryside is flat and occasionally gently undulating.

Leave Kemble station, **turn L** and ride over a stone bridge carrying the road over the railway lines. Follow this road to a T-junction and **turn L**. **Turn R** at the crossroads (signed Cirencester) with the A433. This road can be busy so care is needed but you will not be on it for long.

Soon after passing under a railway bridge (in a dip) look out for two wooden finger posts on the right hand side of the road. Being a dull colour they do not stand out very well. The sign pointing to the left indicates a public footpath to the source of the River Thames, ½ mile away. If you want to visit the source, which is marked by a stone, park your bicycle, cross the stile and follow the path.

After seeing the source, **turn L** back onto the A433. **Turn R** at the crossroads (signed Ewen) onto an unclassified road. At the T-junction with the A429 **turn R** then soon **turn L** (signed Ewen). In Ewen **turn R** at the first T-junction. The river is little more than a stream at this point and winds around to the south of the village. To view it, **turn R** at the T-junction (signed Kemble) and immediately **turn L** (signed Poole Keynes). The river passes under a bridge on the edge of Ewen. Otherwise **turn L** (signed South Cerney). Soon **turn R** (signed Somerford Keynes) past the Flying Duck Inn with its unusual duck clock! **Turn R** at the fork (signed Somerford Keynes).

In Somerford Keynes follow the 'main road' through the village to the crossroads (Neigh Bridge Country Park; toilets and picnic area) and **turn L**. The entrance to the Keynes Country Park is to your left. **Turn R** at the crossroads joining the B4696 (Ashton Keynes) for a short distance then **turn L** at the fork (signed Ashton Keynes).

In Ashton Keynes ride through the village keeping straight on. After passing the memorial in the middle of the village you will see a picturesque scene on the right. There is a stream with stone bridges to the stone-built houses. Ducks populate the stream as is traditional in an English village. Towards the end of the village **turn L** (signed Cricklade). Stay on this road until the crossroads with the B4040 where you **turn L** (signed Cricklade). Ride into Cricklade. Go straight on at the roundabout (signed Town Centre). At the second roundabout the route back to Kemble starts on the B4553 (signed West Swindon).

You might like to take the opportunity to see how the River Thames has grown since Ewen, to visit the impressive church of St Sampson or to visit one of the multitude of eateries in Cricklade. To do this, **turn L** and continue along the main street. After less than ½ mile, on the left hand side of the road is a large sign proudly stating that the River Thames is here. When you have explored to your satisfaction, go back to the roundabout and **turn L** to join the B4553 (signed West Swindon).

Turn R (signed Ashton Keynes) with Broadleaze Farm on the corner. At the crossroads go straight on (Chelworth Lower Green), then **turn L** at the crossroads with the B4040 (signed Malmesbury). Continue straight on at traffic lights at the junction with the B4696. At the crossroads in Minety go straight on (signed Malmesbury/Upper Minety). **Turn R** (signed Oaksey). Following signs for Oaksey ride through Upper Minety until you see

Is it a puddle or is it a river? The Thames near Ewen

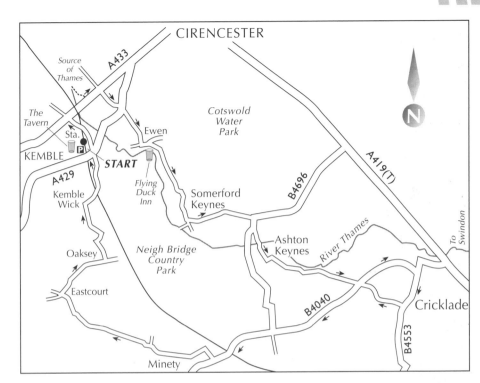

a bus shelter on the right hand side of the road. This bus shelter is close to a T-junction. Keep straight on at this junction (signed Crudwell).

In Eastcourt **turn R** at the crossroads (signed Oaksey) and ride to Oaksey. **Turn R** at the mini roundabout (street name 'The Street'!) to ride into the main part of the village. Just after passing a public house (on the left) **turn L** (signed Kemble) and continue to follow the signs for Kemble.

Just before reaching Kemble the road is carried over a railway line. Soon you will see the church steeple. After passing the church (on the right) **turn R** at the T-junction (signed Cirencester) then **turn L** (signed for Kemble station). At the crossroads with the A429 go straight on, following signs for the station. **Turn L** into Station Road to return to the station and the end of the ride.

THE COTSWOLD WATER PARK

The Cotswold Water Park comprises some 132 lakes covering over 30 square miles of countryside stretching from Lechlade in the east to Kemble in the west. The lakes were formed as a result of gravel extraction and are now a haven for wildlife including rare wildflowers and butterflies, and have developed as an important wintering ground for 16,000 wildfowl from 40 different species. The

Ashton Keynes

lakes also provide a variety of leisure activities including sailing, sail-boarding, water skiing and jet-skiing along with horse riding and fishing. The ride passes by Neigh Bridge and Keynes Country Parks. Both have toilets, picnic facilities and play areas for children. In addition, Keynes Country Park has a lakeside café, a shop, the Jurassic Waterpark fossil exhibition and bicycle hire.

CRICKLADE

Cricklade is the first place of any substance on the banks of the Thames. If you ride along the main street to the river, you will see that it is still little more than a stream, indeed the sign for the river is nearly as wide as the river itself! It may then come as a surprise that, according to the *Anglo Saxon Chronicles*, King Canute arrived by river here in 1016 with a force of some 160 ships! The town has its origins as a Roman settlement of the Dobunni tribe located just west of one of the Romans' major roads, the Ermin Way. In Saxon times, it was a frontier town of Wessex. Since then its history has probably been less exciting, and today the mainly 17th and 18th century buildings on High Street are watched over by the impressive bulk of St Sampson's church (largely 12th century and dedicated to the 6th century wandering Celtic monk-bishop) and its unusual four-turreted tower built by the Duke of Northumberland in 1553.

2

William Morris Country

19 miles

This ride is based on the lovely Thamesside town of Lechlade. The route has a strong arts and crafts theme. We begin by paying homage to Old Father Thames himself at St John's Lock. We then make our way to Kelmscott which towards the latter part of the 19th century became the home of William Morris and the spiritual home of the 'arts and crafts' movement he inspired. The Manor, where he lived, is sometimes open to the public. The ride continues on towards Filkins. Here you can learn about woollen weaving which was the craft, or perhaps I should say the industry, which more than any other moulded the appearance and fortunes of this part of the country.

Map: OS Landranger 163 Cheltenham and Cirencester (GR 214995).

Starting point: The church in the centre of Lechlade. Cars may be parked at the Riverside Park a short distance along the A361 towards Highworth (hourly/daily charges). There is a good picnic area and toilets.

Lechlade has many places to get food and drink. However, the Black Cat Tea Rooms comes highly recommended. The Bell at Langford and the Plough at Kelmscott are good pubs along the route and refreshments are available from the Cotswold Woollen Weavers in Filkins all day except Sunday when it is only open in the afternoon.

The ride is both gentle and flat.

From the church in the centre of Lechlade head in an easterly direction along the A417, St Johns Street (signed Faringdon). After about ½ mile you will reach a bridge over the Thames at St John's Lock, the highest on the river. You can leave your bike and wander down to the lock. Old Father Thames, or at least his statue, is there overseeing the comings and goings and the view of Lechlade church with meadows in the foreground is a pleasant one.

When you are ready, return to the road and retrace your route towards Lechlade. Soon **turn R** (signed Kelmscott). **Turn R** again (signed Kelmscott) and **bear L** into the village. **Turn R** opposite the church and **bear L** by the Plough public house. **Turn R** if you are visiting the Manor, otherwise **turn L**. A short distance out of the village **turn R**

Old Father Thames

and continue on to the crossroads. **Turn R** (signed Clanfield) and remain on this road till it joins the A4095. **Turn L** (signed Clanfield). Ride through the village keeping straight on where the road turns into the B4020.

Just outside the village **turn L** (signed Broadwell). Follow this road (take care with the rough surface) to a T-junction. **Turn R** (signed Broadwell). Continue through Broadwell and Kencot. **Turn L** at the crossroads (signed Filkins). **Turn R** immediately after a left hand turn, Kings Lane, and **turn L** in the village. The Cotswold Woollen Weavers is along this road on your right.

If you have visited the Woollen Weavers, **turn R** back onto the road. **Turn L** (Lamb Inn on the corner) and go straight on at the crossroads (signed Langford). Continue into Langford and **turn R** (signed Little Faringdon). To find the pub or visit the 12th century church you need to continue on into Langford a little further and then go back to the turning. In Little Faringdon, **turn L** (signed Kelmscott). **Turn R** at the T-junction and soon **turn R** again (no signpost, but 10 ton weight limit signs at the road entrance). At the T-junction with the A417 **turn R** and return to Lechlade.

LECHLADE

Lechlade is a pleasant market town centred on a market square of elegant yet functional

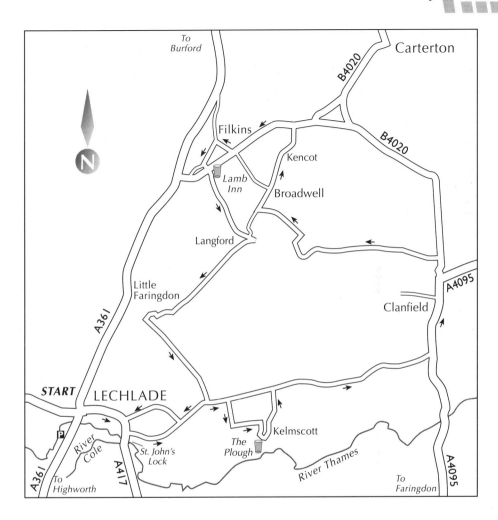

18th and early 19th century buildings. The ride leads you out to Lechlade towards St John's Lock, the highest on the Thames, where you can pay a visit to Old Father Thames, immortalised in concrete by the Victorian sculptor Rafaelle Monti.

KELMSCOTT

Kelmscott is best remembered for William Morris, the craftsman, social philosopher and poet who lived here in the stone Elizabethan manor house from 1871 till his death in 1896. Kelmscott Manor, which he described as a 'heaven on earth', is owned by the Society of Antiquities and is sometimes open to the public. For details, telephone: 01367 252486.

FILKINS

Wool played such an important part in the life of the Cotswolds. Here at Filkins you can visit the Cotswold Woollen Weavers which houses an interesting display about the production of wool in days gone by.

3

Lechlade and the Coln and Leach Valleys

18 miles

This ride explores the picturesque villages and leafy lanes of two delightful tributaries of the Thames, the Leach and the Coln. Take time off to investigate the clapper bridge at Eastleach Martin. Nothing can be more pleasant on a hot day than dangling your feet in the fast moving stream and watching children catching tiddlers. The town of Fairford is located about halfway around the route with its church full of spectacular medieval stained glass and carving and the town providing the possibility of refreshment.

Map: OS Landranger 163 Cheltenham and Cirencester (GR 214995).

Starting point: The church in the centre of Lechlade. Cars may be parked at the Riverside Park a short distance along the A361 towards Highworth (hourly/daily charges). There is a good picnic area and toilets.

This expedition has the possibility of pleasing all the family! Non cyclists will find many interesting walks, especially along the river, and antique shops to explore in Lechlade whilst the cyclists go off on their ride. Lechlade also has many places to get food and drink. The Black Cat Tea Rooms comes highly recommended.

The route is very mixed with some flat, some fairly gentle hills and a short stretch of semi 'off road'.

From the church in the centre of Lechlade head in a northerly direction along the A361. **Turn L** (signed Southrop). Shortly after crossing over the dismantled railway **turn R** at the crossroads (signed Southrop).

Ride into Southrop and **turn R** at the T-junction (signed Southrop). **Bear right** (signed Filkins) at the junction by the Swan public house. **Turn L** (signed Fyfield) and soon

turn L again for the Eastleaches.

Turn L at the fork in Eastleach Martin to ride into the adjoining Eastleach Turville. Just after passing the stone clapper bridge on the left the road swings on a climbing right hand turn.

Keep straight on, following signs for Hatherop, until the road ends at a T-junction. **Turn L** (signed Hatherop). After about ⅓ mile **turn R** (signed

Keble Bridge

Hatherop). Along this road you pass the Macaroni Woods. Do you think that these woods might have been the inspiration for the famous 'spaghetti harvest' April Fools' joke? At the T-junction **turn R** and ride into Hatherop. In the village **turn L** (signed Coln St Aldwyns). Ride into the centre of Coln St Aldwyns and **turn L** (signed Quenington). In Quenington keep straight on at the crossroads (signed Fairford). Keep straight on at the next two junctions at the side of the village green.

After about 2 miles **turn L** in a village called Milton End, now signed as part of Fairford. There is no signpost but look out for a stone-built tower with a pitched roof in the corner of a field on the left,

then turn, following the stone wall. Shortly after crossing a bridge over a stream (do pause here and admire the tranquil scene), enter Fairford. **Turn R** into High Street. Pay a visit to the church on the right, famous for its stained glass windows.

Continue along High Street until the T-junction with the A417. **Turn R again** (signed Cirencester). Take care on this junction as the view is partly obscured. Shortly after re-crossing the stream **turn L** (signed Horcott Industrial Estate). Ride through Horcott and pass by the entrance to the RAF Fairford airbase then at the T-junction in Whelford **turn L** (signed Lechlade).

Very soon after Whelford **turn R** onto a narrow road (signed

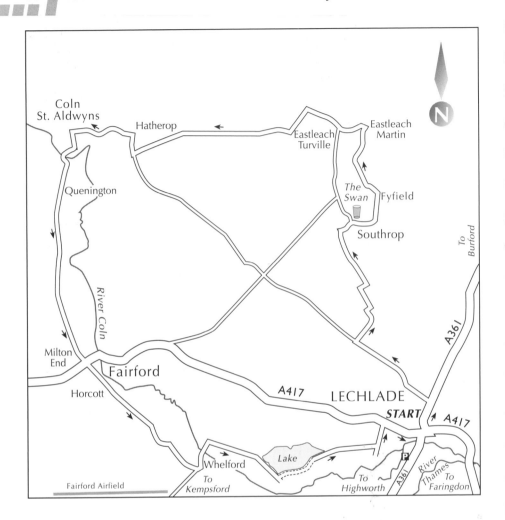

Dudgrove, No Through Road). **Turn L** onto a small gravel road (no signs) skirting around a lake belonging to the Cotswold Water Park. If you cross a small bridge you have overshot; turn around and you will see the gravel road on your right. The road is a little rough but quite rideable. If you prefer, stay on the road signposted to Lechlade when you leave Whelford.

Follow the road until it joins the A417 in Lechlade and **turn R** to ride back into the town centre. For anyone interested in canals, there is a footpath off to the right about ¼ mile before the gravel road joins the A417. This leads to the confluence of the rivers Thames and Coln and is also the place where the now abandoned Severn and Thames Canal joined the Thames. You can still see the lock keeper's round house.

. . . .

FAIRFORD

The history of this town lying on the banks of the River Coln stretch back at least until Anglo Saxon times. The town was undoubtedly in its heyday during the late medieval period when its wealth, like that of many Cotswold towns, was built on the wool trade. The magnificent church of St Mary, built in the late Perpendicular style, was founded by John Tame and his son Edmund who were part of one of the Cotswolds' most wealthy families of wool merchants. The stained glass, parts of which illustrate graphically the medieval obsession with the tortures meted out in hell, is the work of Flemish craftsman Bernard Flower. Look out for the Devil (who is blue!) wheeling the damned around in a wheelbarrow! Personally, I love the carvings on the underneath of the misericords in the choir. These tip-up seats were designed originally for infirm monks to perch against so they could keep to the spirit, if not the rule, of St Benedict that all monks should sing the daily offices standing up. The carvings are very vivid and illustrate scenes of medieval life.

EASTLEACH MARTIN AND EASTLEACH TURVILLE

These two villages straddle the River Leach, their churches facing each other across the water. The larger of the two belongs to Eastleach Martin. However, the smaller is the more interesting with a 14th century saddleback roof, Norman tympanum and 13th century interior. The clapper bridge over the Leach is known locally as Keble Bridge and is a lovely spot, especially on quiet weekdays in summer. In spring the two villages are clothed in daffodils.

4

Bampton – In the Footsteps of Mammoths

22 miles

We start in the peaceful and elegant town of Bampton. Take some time to explore the magnificent church and side streets full of stone cottages. The route then heads east into the Thames floodplain. The scenery here has been created by the river. Drainage ditches and small brooks criss-cross the fields and before long the route emerges next to the flooded gravel workings. These are a feature of this part of the Thames Valley and provide a haven for both wildfowl and fishermen. These riverside gravel beds have preserved many previous inhabitants of the area including mammoths.

The village of Stanton Harcourt is a natural stopping point. Its manor house and medieval Pope's Tower are sometimes open to the public. For those of you interested in wildlife, the Vicarage Pit Nature Reserve may reward you with glimpses of cormorants, grebes and numerous other water birds.

Map: Landranger 164 Oxford, Chipping Norton and Bicester (GR 314032).

Starting point: The square in the centre of Bampton. Cars may be parked in the central square and on Broad Street (for a maximum of 4 hours) and there are public toilets close by.

If you wish to eat in Bampton, the Romany Inn on Bridge Street is highly recommended. Other good alternatives are the Red Lion in Northmoor or the Fox in Stanton Harcourt. There is a shop in Bampton's square which is open seven days a week and is convenient for buying snacks and drinks.

This is an ideal ride for those wanting to reacquaint themselves with cycling. There is plenty of interest along the way and the route is flat and uses mostly quiet roads and tracks.

From the square, head east along High Street. After the Morris Clown pub **bear R** (signed Buckland). After 1¾ miles **turn L** (signed Chimney). At the T-junction **turn L** and cross the drainage ditch on a bridge. Soon turn R (signed Cote). At the T-junction in Cote **turn R** (signed Old Shifford). The road narrows and is eventually unfenced. On your right you will pass Shifford church, now some distance from the village.

Stanton Harcourt Manor House and Pope's Tower

Proceed to the junction with the B4449. **Turn R** (no signpost). Continue for about 1 mile and then **turn R** onto the A415. **Turn L** into the centre of Standlake. Soon you will pass the entrance to a campsite and pub on the right.

Bear R in the village (signed Stanton Harcourt) and follow the road, crossing the River Windrush. You are now a mile above its confluence with the River Thames at Newbridge. **Turn R** (signed Northmoor) on a sharp left hand bend. One mile beyond Northmoor village you will see a right hand turn (signed Bablock Hythe). A regular ferry service used to operate from the Ferry Inn (there is now an irregular one!). If you like you can make a short detour down to the pub to enjoy a pint on its riverside terrace. Otherwise carry straight on and **turn R** (signed Stanton Harcourt).

Continue through the village. The church and manor house are on your right. **Turn R** by the Fox public house (New Road). **Turn L** in Sutton and **turn L** once again at the junction with the B4449 (no signpost). Follow this road going straight across at the roundabout. The lake of the Vicarage Pit Nature Reserve (owned by the Berks, Bucks and Oxon Naturalists Trust) is ½ mile along the road on the right.

Go straight over at the crossroads with the A415 (signed Yelford).

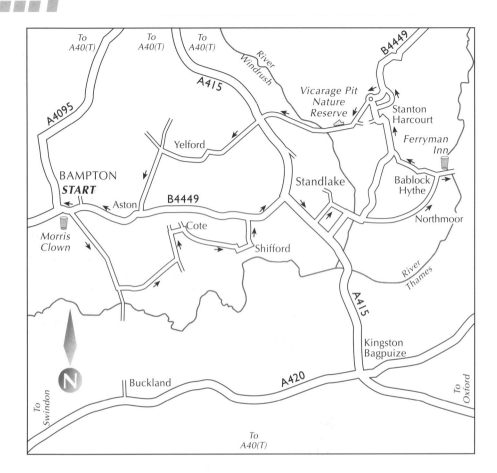

Follow this road up a short rise and down a hill through the hamlet of Yelford. Continue till you reach a crossroads. **Turn L** (signed Aston). In Aston **turn R** (signed Bampton). You will shortly pass the Aston Pottery on your right. On entering Bampton **turn R** back along High Street to return to the main square.

BAMPTON

Today Bampton is a quiet market town full of 17th and 18th century mellow stone houses and several old coaching inns, one of which, the Morris Clown, still bears a notice 'Grooming, Posting House and Livery Stables'. The church dominates the views in the flat Thames floodplain, its spire reaching an impressive 170 ft. The church and graveyard are well worth exploring. The town still feels slightly isolated. Perhaps this is left over from the times when Bampton could not be reached by road during the winter and for that reason it was known as Bampton in the Bush.

The church with no village, Old Shifford

STANTON HARCOURT

This is a pretty village full of thatched cottages and handsome town houses. The medieval manor house includes a tower, built in 1470 and known as Pope's Tower because the poet stayed there in 1718 whilst translating Homer. The manor house and grounds are open to the public at regular intervals.

The nearby gravel workings have given a rare insight into the fauna and conditions during one of the interglacial periods some 200,000 years ago. Finds include some 700 bones and teeth of large animals: bison, horse, mammoth, bear and hyena. Some early human tools have also been recovered. All were deposited in silts, sands and gravels by what is thought to have been the ancient Thames at a time when it was confluent with the River Rhine, and Britain was still joined by a land bridge to mainland Europe. The discoveries of mammoths is baffling, firstly because the species found here is much smaller than usual (even though some of the tusks were 3 metres long!) and secondly because the climate during this interglacial was much warmer than would usually support mammoths. Some of the discoveries may be viewed in the Natural History Museum in Oxford.

5

The Windrush and the Evenlode

23 miles

This ride features two of the Thames' many tributaries, the Windrush and the Evenlode. The Windrush is a beautifully descriptive name for the river which starts its life as a trickle, high above the village of Cutsdean, and grows to flow through some of the most beautiful Cotswold towns and villages, for example, Bourton-on-the-Water and Burford, before reaching the town of Witney where our ride begins. It then turns south to meet the Thames at Newbridge, a total journey of 60 miles. Our ride follows the river to the picturesque village of Minster Lovell with its ruined manor house, a place of romantic legends.

We then turn north to Leafield and through what remains of the once great hunting forest of Wychwood to Charlbury where we meet our second tributary, the Evenlode. This river starts its journey to the Thames further north, rising in the hills above Moreton-in-Marsh. We ride through the valley it has shaped, passing the large 4th century Romano-British villa near East End as we go. We now swing south and return to Witney via Cogges Manor Farm Museum to pay homage to Victorian farming, and possibly also to enjoy some tea and cakes.

Map: OS Landranger 164 Oxford, Chipping Norton and Bicester (GR 356096).

Starting point: This ride starts from the Butter Cross in the centre of Witney some 14 miles west of Oxford. There is no railway station, but if you wish to travel by train you may join the ride at Charlbury which is on the line between Oxford and Worcester. If you travel to Witney by car, there is a car park on Welch Way, just off High Street.

Good food may be found at many pubs along the route – Charlbury is said to have boasted over 20 at one time! In particular, the Bell Hotel in Charlbury, the Masons Arms in North Leigh and the White Hart in Minster Lovell (off the route on the B4047) are all recommended.

The ride is an undulating one, indeed it is seldom flat. However, there are many lovely views of the two valleys, and the few short, sharp climbs are all on quiet roads with plenty to look at.

The ruined manor house, Minster Lovell

From the Butter Cross, **turn R** at the mini roundabout and head onto High Street. Continue straight across at two further mini roundabouts and one set of traffic lights. **Turn L** at the double mini roundabout (B4022, signed Hailey). Go straight across at the mini roundabout (signed Crawley). In Crawley **turn R** and immediately **turn L** (signed Minster Lovell, Oxfordshire Cycleway). **Turn L** at the fork (signed Minster Lovell). Below and to your left runs the Windrush. Soon you will see the church, ruined hall and dovecote. If you wish to visit them **turn L** soon after entering the village (signed to the church). Otherwise keep straight on into the village proper.

Turn R at the T-junction by the Old Swan Inn (no signpost). Climb a hill and **turn L** (signed Asthall Leigh). **Turn R** at the T-junction in Asthall Leigh (signed Fordwells) and descend through a pretty valley. **Bear R** in the village (signed Leafield). **Turn L** at the T-junction (signed Leafield) and climb the hill into the village. **Turn R** with the village green on your left. **Turn R** onto the 'main road'.

Turn L (signed Chadlington) onto a beautiful road which skirts the edge of Wychwood Forest. Continue on this road for nearly 3 miles until it reaches a T-junction. **Turn R** (signed Charlbury) and descend past the railway station, over the River Evenlode and into the town of

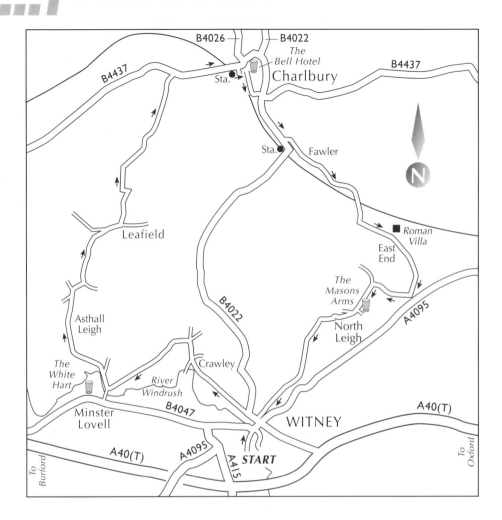

Charlbury. **Turn R** (Church Lane, No Through Road). Ahead of you to your left are the gates of the churchyard. Dismount and walk through. If you want to explore Charlbury then **turn L**, otherwise **turn R**.

Descend initially and then climb. **Turn R** on the main road and immediately **turn R** again (Fawler Road, B4022). After about a mile turn L (signed Fawler). Continue into the village and **bear R** (signed North Leigh). **Turn R** and cross the railway and descend to cross the Evenlode once again. Immediately afterwards **turn L** (signed East End) and climb steeply with the river winding eccentrically to your left. Just after passing the East End village sign, to your left is the bridle path to the Roman Villa (a detour of ¾ mile).

Our route continues through East End. **Turn R** at the T-junction (signed Wilcote). Descend the hill and **turn L** (signed North Leigh). Climb through the village to the T-junction at the top of the hill. **Turn R** (New Yatt Road) and follow this road through New Yatt and into the outskirts of Witney. **Turn R** onto the A4095. Follow signs for Witney town centre and the Tourist Information Centre. This will return you to the Butter Cross.

If you want to visit Cogges Manor Farm Museum. Follow the town centre signs as far as the traffic lights. **Turn L** (Witan Way). Proceed to the next roundabout. As you approach the roundabout, stop and get onto the footpath. To your left your should see a blue footpath sign for Cogges Manor Farm. Follow it over a bridge, past the entrance to a churchyard and **turn R** when the path forks. Cogges Manor Farm entrance is ahead of you on the right.

MINSTER LOVELL HALL

Minster Lovell is a place of legends, and if you find yourself alone on a quiet afternoon walking amid the ruined banqueting hall and kitchen ranges of the 15th century manor house on the banks of the Windrush, you might find yourself believing them. The ruins are of a fortified manor house built along with the adjoining church of St Kenhelm by

William, seventh baron of Minster Lovell, around 1431. The most famous legend concerns Francis, the ninth baron, who was a favourite of Richard III. After fighting on Richard's side at Bosworth he fled and subsequently joined the forces of Lambert Simnel who claimed to be Edward, Earl of Warwick and rightful heir to the throne. After an unsuccessful battle against the forces of Henry VII, Francis fled across the River Trent. Some say he was drowned, but others claim he made it back to Minster Lovell and hid in a secret room known only to one faithful servant, who brought him food. This story was regarded as just a legend until, in 1708 during repairs to the house, workmen made a grim discovery. Hidden in a secret room behind a great chimney stack was the skeleton of a man and a small dog. History or legend . . . what do you think?

COGGES MANOR FARM, WITNEY

This working farm museum is located in a beautiful 700 year old stone manor house in Cogges, a hamlet now on the edge of Witney. Here you can discover what life was like in rural Oxfordshire during the Victorian era. At weekends there are numerous displays and demonstrations varying from lacemaking and bookbinding to steam threshing and falconry. There is also a wide range of farm animals as well as walks in the adjoining kitchen garden and fields. The farm is open on Tuesday to Friday from 10.30 am to 5.30 pm and on Saturdays from 12 noon to 5.30 pm between the end of March and the end of October. An entrance fee is charged.

6

Circumnavigating Port Meadow

8 miles or 9 miles

This ride explores the waterways north of Oxford. The route leaves Oxford along the Oxford Canal as far as Wolvercote. It continues along the northern margin of Port Meadow to Godstow where it picks up the Thames towpath for a while before visiting the hamlet of Binsey, its church and sacred well.

The route circumnavigates Port Meadow, a lovely area of common land which is still grazed by cattle and horses. In early summer it is a sea of yellow buttercups. In winter it floods and in particularly cold winters it freezes and turns into an impromptu ice rink. In what is probably an apocryphal tale an American tourist is supposed to have asked an Oxford don to take him to see the oldest remains in Oxford and was surprised to be taken to Port Meadow. Here, evidence of habitation stretching back to the Bronze Age has been found. It was mentioned in the Domesday Book as a place where all freemen of Oxford could graze animals outside the city walls. Today, as you will see, it is a popular place for walkers, rowers, runners kite flyers and model aircraft enthusiasts.

Map: OS Landranger 164 Oxford, Chipping Norton and Bicester (GR 505063 Oxford railway station; GR 492063 Seacourt Park and Ride).

Starting point: There is a choice of starting points, either the Seacourt Park and Ride located on Botley Road near the junction of the A34 and A420 to the west of Oxford, or the Oxford railway station.

There are several pleasant riverside pubs on this route including the Perch at Binsey and the Trout at Godstow.

This route is flat and about half of it is on canal or river towpaths. The surface of the paths is generally good, although after heavy rain some sections may be muddy. The towpaths are informal cycle routes and are shared with walkers and fishermen – please be considerate to other users. For those wanting a longer ride, this circuit can be linked with Route 7.

Starting from Oxford railway station (8 miles)
Exit the main station entrance (on platform 1) and proceed down the road, leaving the station. **Turn L** onto the main road for a short distance, then **turn L** at the traffic lights (Rewley Road). Follow this

Riding along the towpath of the Oxford Canal

The Thames flowing through Port Meadow, Oxford

road through the new housing development and immediately after the bridge over the river cutting **turn R** along a track which leads via a bridge to the Oxford Canal towpath.

Turn L along the towpath (signed Banbury). Continue for approximately 2 miles. For most of the time, Port Meadow is hidden to your left. Cross under the railway bridge and proceed to the following bridge (Bridge 236). Push your bike over and cross Wolvercote Green, coming out opposite the Plough public house.

Turn L onto Wolvercote Green Road and at the T-junction **turn L** (Godstow Road). Follow the road as it winds through Wolvercote. On a

sharp right hand bend you will come across one of the traditional bathing places with toilets, a car park and picnic area. On the nearby bridge you will see a memorial to the crew of a monoplane which crashed nearby in 1912 when the meadow was used by the Royal Flying Corps for training purposes. You are now at the northern end of the meadow and the famous 'dreaming spires' can be seen in the distance.

Just along the road is the Trout public house, a popular watering hole which those of you familiar with Inspector Morse may just recognise. Cross the Thames on the narrow road bridge, and immediately after **turn L** through a gate onto the river towpath (signed

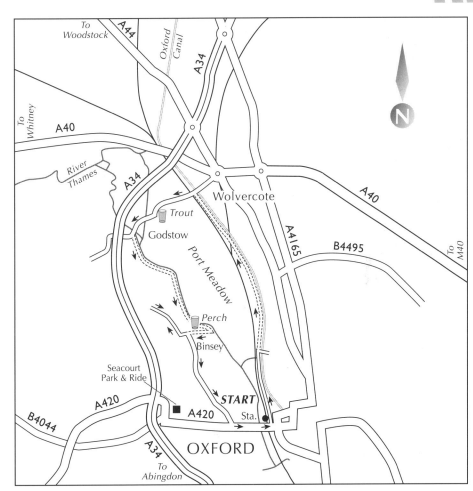

Thames Path, Osney). The ruined building on your right is Godstow Nunnery. Push your bike when beside the lock and continue along the riverside path. There are several gates on this section.

After nearly 1 mile you will come to a gravel and concrete track off to the right, just before a boatyard. **Turn R** along the gravel and concrete road in the direction of some houses (Binsey village). Push

your bike through the kissing gate and **bear R** along the road by the houses. Continue on till the road ends at a 'Private Road' notice. Follow the path to your left into the churchyard. At the west end of the churchyard is St Margaret's Well, known locally as the Treacle Well and immortalised by Lewis Carroll in *Alice's Adventures in Wonderland*.

When you are ready, retrace your steps back to Binsey village and the kissing gate, but continue on the road back into West Oxford.* **Turn L** onto Botley Road to return to the station.

Starting from the Seacourt Park and Ride (9 miles)

Leave the Park and Ride and return to the junction with the main (Botley) road. **Turn L** onto the pavement cycle track. Continue along till you join the main route at the railway station. Follow the main route as far as *. Cross Botley Road at the pedestrian crossing (to your right). **Turn R** on the cycle track and return to the Park and Ride (½ mile).

THE OXFORD CANAL

In the early years of the canal boom, the Oxford Canal was one of the most important in the south of England as it joined the Warwickshire coalfields to Banbury and Oxford and also provided a link to the River Thames. It was begun in 1769 by James Brindley who designed it as a contour canal, deliberately following a winding path to minimise the number of locks. The result is that the Oxford to Banbury stretch, 19 miles by road, is 27 miles by canal. It was soon overtaken in importance by the Grand Union Canal linking London and Birmingham. However, the shareholders still made a good return on their investment by dint of charging exorbitant tolls for the 5½ mile section which linked the Birmingham canal network to the Grand Union Canal. Today life on the Oxford Canal hums to a gentle tune with a pleasing mixture of barges in long term mooring and leisure craft and plenty of ducks, coots, moorhens, herons, dabchicks and even the odd water rat to look out for as you ride along.

GODSTOW NUNNERY

The ruins that now grace the banks of the river at Godstow were once a Benedictine nunnery boasting a magnificent church, courts, cloisters and chapter house, and inhabited by well connected nuns. However, it was a place of scandal. King Henry II's mistress, Rosalind Clifford, was a nun here, and it is reputed that she was buried within the Nunnery. In Aubrey's *Natural History of Oxfordshire* there is a description of her grave being excavated: 'Not long since her grave was digged, where some of her bones were found, and her teeth so white (as ye dwellers there report) that beholders did much wonder at them'. Not surprisingly, the ruins are supposed to be haunted. Later the place became notorious for the 'hospitality' it offered to the monks of Oxford, and it was demolished in 1541 as part of Henry VIII's dissolution of the monasteries.

ST MARGARET'S WELL, BINSEY

The provision of St Margaret's Well in the churchyard at Binsey is said to have been a miracle resulting from the prayers of St Frideswide. Its alternative name, Treacle Well, refers to the medieval meaning of treacle, a healing liquid. The author Lewis Carroll knew this spot well and incorporated it (taking its modern meaning) in his tales of Alice.

7

Exploring the Isis

8 miles or 10 miles

This ride explores the Thames (or Isis as it is known within Oxford). Much of the ride is off road on cycle tracks and towpath and it offers an interesting view of a lesser known side of Oxford. It passes along quiet meadows at the back of Christchurch and Merton Colleges. You will see the college boathouses and during term-time the river between Folly Bridge and Donnington Bridge is often busy with rowing eights. In spring, some of these meadows are awash with purple fritillaries. The route leaves the river at Iffley Lock and explores Iffley village with its rare Romanesque church. Return to Oxford over Magdalen Bridge, the scene of mass celebrations each May Day. You are now in the heart of the University City, so why not take time off from the route to explore some of the colleges or museums?

Map: OS Landranger 164 Oxford, Chipping Norton and Bicester (GR 505063 Oxford railway station; GR 492063 Seacourt Park and Ride).

Starting point: There is a choice of starting points, either the Seacourt Park and Ride located on Botley Road near the junction of the A34 and A420 to the west of Oxford, or the Oxford railway station.

There are plenty of pubs en route and in the summer ice-creams and cold drinks are available at Iffley Lock.

Much of this route is on cycle track and river towpath. The towpath is generally in good condition, although the section between Folly Bridge and Donnington Bridge can become muddy in the winter. The river towpath is an informal cycle path and is popular with walkers. Please be considerate to them. There are no hills, but be prepared to get off and push your bike across the locks. For those wanting a longer ride, this circuit can be linked with Route 6.

Starting from Oxford railway station (8 miles)

If you arrive by train on platforms 1 or 3, use the main station exit and push your bike over the pedestrian bridge joining the station to the car park. Don't go into the car park, but down the slope and **turn L** into the side street and immediately **turn L** onto Botley Road so that you pass under the bridge you have just crossed and the railway line. If you

The Radcliffe Camera, Oxford

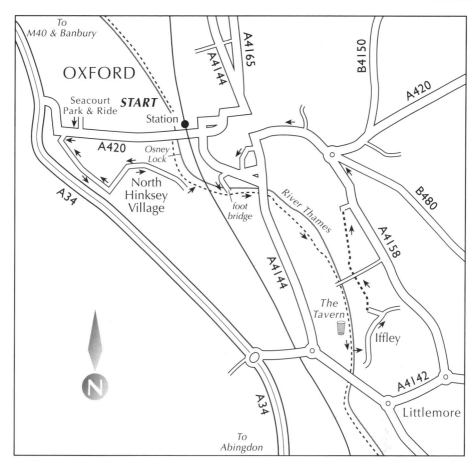

arrive on platform 2, leave the station via the 'West Oxford' exit. Go down the slope and **turn R** onto Botley Road.

Once on Botley Road, **turn L** immediately after crossing the river. Cross the bridge and **turn L** (North Street). Follow the road round to the right to ride parallel to the river and join the towpath opposite the Waterman's Arms. Continue to Osney Lock (no cycling).* Continue along the towpath for about a mile until it crosses Abingdon Road at Folly Bridge

(near the Head of the River pub). Take care and cross the road.

Get back onto the towpath, the river to your left. This section of the river is used for the inter-college 'bump' rowing races which are held in March and June. During term-time you will often see rowing eights training along this stretch, their coaches cycling up and down the towpath! The majority of college boathouses are on the far side of the river. Continue, passing under Donnington Bridge to Iffley Lock (no cycling). Cross over the

The Thames towpath, opposite the college boathouses at Oxford

river via the modern lock and the remains of the original pound lock and **turn L** up a short rise into Iffley village. Pass Grist Cottage with mill stones embedded in its walls and **turn R** onto Mill Lane. Continue round to the church.

From the churchyard entrance, go straight along Church Way. Note the Old Parochial School (now the village hall) on your left. **Turn L** (Meadow Lane) and continue, crossing Donnington Bridge Road (care!). Go on to the T-junction. **Turn R** (Jackdaw Lane) and **turn L** (Iffley Road). Go straight over the Plain Roundabout and onto Magdalen Bridge. Magdalen Tower is straight ahead of you. Just over the bridge to your left is the

entrance to the University Botanical Gardens, a tranquil haven on any day. Keep straight on at traffic lights and enter High Street.

At Carfax crossroads, **bear L** down St Aldates. Just past the imposing entrance to Christchurch College (on your left), **turn R** (Brewer Street). Along here, the birthplace of the author Dorothy L. Sayers (best known for her detective story writing) is marked by a blue plaque. **Turn L** at the T-junction (Littlegate Street) and at the bottom of the hill where the road curves to the left, **bear R** onto the cycle track (Faulkner Street, No Through Road!).

Keep following signs for the South Oxford Cycle Route. You will **bear R** along a red brick path to a set of pedestrian lights crossing a main road. Cross here and continue following the blue signs into Blackfriars Road, and cross the river on the footbridge. As you exit the bridge, **turn L** (signed West Oxford). Return along the towpath **, and cross Osney Lock. Rejoin East Street by the Waterman's Arms and **bear L** into North Street. **Turn R** over the bridge and **turn R** onto Botley Road. **Turn L** into the station at the traffic lights.

Starting from the Seacourt Park and Ride (10 miles)
On leaving the Park and Ride cross Botley Road and **turn R** onto the cycle track on the other side. **Turn L** (signed North Hinksey) and at the T-junction **turn L** (North Hinksey Lane). After about ½ mile **turn L** along the cycle track (signed City Centre). Follow this track till it meets the road at a mini roundabout. Go straight over into the industrial estate. **Turn L** along the cycle track (signed City Centre) and continue to meet the Thames towpath. **Turn R** (signed City Centre).

You are now on the main route at *. Follow until **. Just before the bridge leading to Osney Lock **turn L** down the cycle path (no signpost). At the junction with the road **turn R** and proceed to the mini roundabout. Go straight over onto the cycle track. **Turn R** onto North Hinksey Lane and retrace your route to the Park and Ride.

OXFORD

When you are on High Street, you are in the heart of the University City. Take some time off to explore before rejoining the ride. The University consists of some 35 colleges, each of which is a separate and self-governing institution. The colleges vary greatly in age and in character. Most of them open their grounds free to visitors; look out for notices in the porters' lodges. Just off to your right as you ride down High Street is Radcliffe Square, enclosed by the University Church, Brasenose and All Souls Colleges and the Bodleian Library buildings. In its centre stands the Radcliffe Camera. Oxford boasts some interesting museums: the Ashmolean Museum (the oldest public museum in the country) housing art and artefacts from all around the world, the University Museum (natural history), a wonderful example of Victorian public building design, the History of Science Museum, the Pitt Rivers Collection, the Museum of Oxford and the Oxford Story to name just a few. There are plenty of eating places to suit every palate.

IFFLEY

The village of Iffley lies about 3 miles from the centre of Oxford and is now enclosed within the city limits. A lock over the Thames, known as a pound lock, was first constructed in the late 17th century, one of the earliest built on the river. The modern lock is a popular destination for walkers and rowers alike. The 12th century church is unusual because it has retained its original design. It is constructed in the grand style of the late Romanesque period (around 1175) and is rich in both internal and external carving of exquisite detail.

8

Woodstock and the Northern Tributaries

23 miles

This ride starts out from the scenic and historic town of Woodstock and meanders around some interesting and picturesque villages lying on the Thames' northern tributaries, the Glyme and Cherwell. This countryside is dominated by stately homes and their surrounding lands and estate villages. Blenheim Palace at Woodstock has grounds which take up nine square miles to the west and north of the town. The privately owned Glympton Park may be glimpsed as you descend into its estate village of Glympton and Rousham House, with its beautiful and historically interesting gardens stretching to the banks of the Cherwell, may be visited on the course of the ride.

Map: OS Landranger 164 Oxford, Chipping Norton and Bicester (GR 447167).

Starting point: This ride starts from the A44 in Woodstock some 8 miles north of Oxford. The town cannot be reached by train, but the nearest station is Long Hanborough, 3 miles to the west, on the line from Oxford to Worcester. There is a well-signed and large pay and display car park by the library and police station, off Hensington Road.

Woodstock is well endowed with pubs and teashops. We recommend Harriet's Teashop on High Street and the King's Head pub on Park Lane. The County Museum also has a coffee shop. Halfway around the route we can recommend the White Horse in Duns Tew. Alternatively you can picnic among the hedges and classical statues of the Rousham Park.

The ride is an undulating one, and there are a couple of steepish (though short) climbs and descents into and out of the Glyme and Cherwell valleys. The villages you pass through are all delightful and are well worth taking the time to explore.

From the main A44, take Hensington Road (signed Tackley). Shortly and on a right hand bend **turn L** (signed Tackley, Banbury Road). After rounding a sharpish left hand bend look to your left and you will see the Column of Victory, located within the grounds of Blenheim Palace. At the T-junction **turn L** (signed Wootton/Chipping Norton). **Turn L** again at the next junction (there is no signpost, but

Blenheim Palace, Woodstock

the Oxford School of Drama is immediately on your left after you turn). The road dips down and passes over the River Glyme before rising out of the valley again. At the next junction, within sight of the A44, **turn R** (signed Wootton). **Turn R** again at the T-junction (signed Wootton).

At the bottom of the descent into Wootton the route passes over the River Glyme again. The climb into the rest of the village is twisting and steep, but in the summer the cottage gardens along this stretch are a delight. Stay on the 'main' road, passing the church on the right and then the village well on your left.

At the T-junction (the Killingworth Castle pub is on the corner) **turn L** (signed Glympton). At the fork **bear L** staying on the 'main' road (signed Glympton). The descent into the village is quite steep and as you swoop down you look down on the roof of Glympton Park itself. As you ride into Glympton our old friend the River Glyme flows alongside the road. In the village the road bends sharply to the left. On this bend **turn R** (signed The Bartons). Close by is an old set of stocks and a seat.

Climb out of the valley then **turn L** at the crossroads (signed The Bartons/Sandford). At the crossroads **turn R** (signed The Bartons). Keep straight on at the next junction (signed Middle Barton). You should

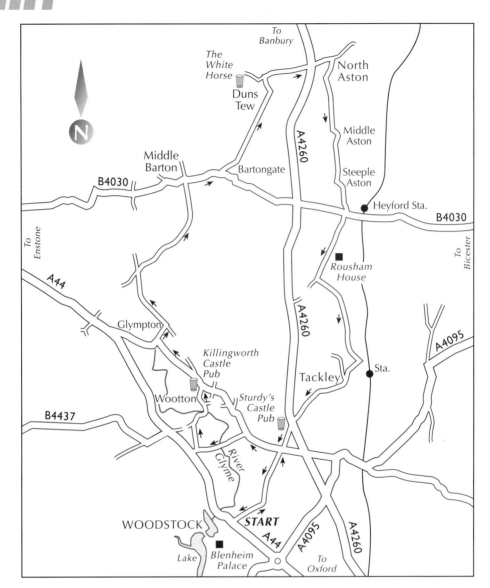

now enjoy another spectacular descent, into the village of Middle Barton (signed The Bartons). Here **turn R** at the crossroads (signed The Heyfords/Bicester, B4030). **Turn L** (signed Duns Tew).

Turn L at the T-junction (signed Duns Tew). Duns Tew is a wonderful mixture of grey Cotswold stone and orange/brown ironstone buildings. If you wish to sample the hospitality of the White Horse, then **turn L** at the T-junction opposite the church, otherwise **turn R** (signed North Aston).

Longhorn cattle in the grounds of Rousham Park

At the crossroads with the A4260 go straight over (signed North Aston). In North Aston **turn R** (signed Middle Aston). **Turn L** at the T-junction (signed Middle Aston House). Ride into Steeple Aston and **turn L** at the T-junction (no signpost, but the post office and village shop is on the corner). The road descends steeply with some bends so take care as you ride down. At the bottom of the descent go straight over at the crossroads with traffic lights (signed Rousham). The entrance to Rousham House and its landscaped gardens is shortly to your left.

After Rousham **turn L** (signed Nethercott/Tackley). Ride into Tackley (another fine stone village) and stay on the 'main' road. The steep climb out of the village is the last one on this ride, and that is a promise! At the T-junction **turn L** (signed Kidlington, A4260) and immediately **turn R** (signed Woodstock) passing the pub called Sturdy's Castle. Go straight over at the crossroads (signed Hensington). This road will take you back to Woodstock where it becomes Hensington Road.

WOODSTOCK AND BLENHEIM PALACE

The town of Woodstock was a royal manor before the Norman Conquest and therefore the town and its adjoining park have ancient royal roots. Henry I enclosed the park for hunting and Henry II enlarged the original palace and built 'New Woodstock' to house his court. The medieval palace continued to be used by succeeding monarchs, but was destroyed beyond repair during the Civil War. In 1704, the manor and park were given to the first Duke of Marlborough by Queen Anne, in gratitude for his victory at Blenheim. The house was designed by Vanbrugh and built over the period 1705–1722. The 2,500 acre estate was landscaped by Capability Brown about 50 years later. The River Glyme is used to feed several magnificent lakes. The house contains many interesting treasures including carvings by Grinling Gibbons and an amazing series of Belgian tapestries depicting scenes from the Battle of Blenheim. The house is open from March to the end of October, and the grounds are open all year. An entrance fee is charged for both.

Woodstock is also home to the Oxfordshire County Museum which along with permanent displays on the history and life on the county also has a series of changing exhibitions.

ROUSHAM PARK

Rousham House was built in 1635 by Sir Robert Dormer and is still in the ownership of the same family. William Kent added the wings and stable block around 1738. The house was extensively redecorated in the 18th century, although significant features from the earlier Jacobean house remain. From a historical perspective, the most important feature of the park is its gardens which descend gently to the banks of the River Cherwell. They are today perhaps the earliest unaltered example of English landscape design and also one of the best preserved works of William Kent. The gardens were set out as a series of terraces with fountains, cascades, statues and buildings in the Italian taste. The views are skilfully manipulated by the use of hedges and trees to provide what seems like a series of garden tableaux. The house is open on Wednesdays and Sundays (and Bank Holiday Mondays) from April to September, 2 pm to 4.30 pm. The gardens are open daily, 10 am to 4.30 pm. No children under 15 or dogs.

9

The Only Ford on the Thames

28 miles

This route starts and finishes at the historic Thamesside market town of Abingdon. Initially, it follows the Thames. The river soon heads north to loop around the hills south-west of Oxford, but we head over Boars Hill to rejoin the river after its excursion. The route continues on a ridge looking down on the river until at Hinton Waldrist it heads down to Duxford to the only ford on the Thames. It returns to Abingdon via Fyfield and Gozzards Ford.

Map: OS Landranger 164 Oxford, Chipping Norton and Bicester (GR 501968).

Starting point: The route starts from the car parks immediately south of the river bridge on the A415 at Abingdon, 8 miles south of Oxford. Abingdon cannot be reached by train. The nearest railway station is Radley, 3 miles away, on the line between Oxford and Didcot. If you travel by train you may pick the route up outside Radley College, on the road from Radley to Kennington.

Refreshments of every sort are available in Abingdon. There are two cafés near the bridge over the Thames – the Gallery Tea Rooms on Bridge Street and also in the Old Gaol Leisure Centre which is set back from Bridge Street in its own courtyard. The ford at Duxford is a lovely place to have a picnic in fine weather. The Blue Boar at Longworth is a good pub for food.

This route is mainly flat, but there is one significant climb up to Boars Hill.

Turn out of your car park and cross the bridge over the Thames. After a short distance there is a give way line. To your right is the Abbey Archway. Stop, cross the road and go under the archway. **Turn R** (Abbey Close). Follow the road until you have crossed the Abbey Stream on a small bridge. **Turn L** onto the gravel track next to the stream. Continue till you reach a wooden footbridge. Re-cross the stream and follow the track (signed Barton Court). On reaching the tarmac road, **bear R** and immediately **bear L**, keeping the Abbey Centre on your left. **Turn R** at the T-junction and continue to the roundabout.

Turn R (signed Radley). **Turn L** (White's Lane). Continue past the entrance to Radley College and after

The Abbey Gate, Abingdon

½ mile **turn L** (Sugworth Lane). Go straight on at the staggered crossorads (signed Sunningwell). Continue into the village and stop by the church (with its unique seven-sided porch) and village pond. This is a picturesque place to pause for a breather, otherwise retrace your route for 50 yards and **turn L** (signed Bayworth).

Bear L in Bayworth village (signed Boars Hill) and soon you will find yourself climbing up a steep (though short) wooded hill. **Turn L** at the T-junction (signed Old Boars Hill) and soon **turn R** (signed Old Boars Hill). To your right, good views can be obtained of the 'dreaming spires' of Oxford. Follow the road until it narrows to a single track. Soon after, on your right is Jarn Mound. You can climb the steps to the viewpoint, or walk a couple of hundred yards to Matthew Arnold's Field. There are plenty of spots for a picnic or a rest after your climb.

On leaving, head down the hill. At the T-junction **turn L** (signed Lower Wootton). Soon, cross straight over at the staggered crossorads (signed Bessels Leigh) and continue till you reach the A420. **Turn L** and immediately **turn R** by the Greyhound pub (care!). Continue through the village and **turn L** at the next junction (signed Eaton and Appleton).

Bear L along the straight road to

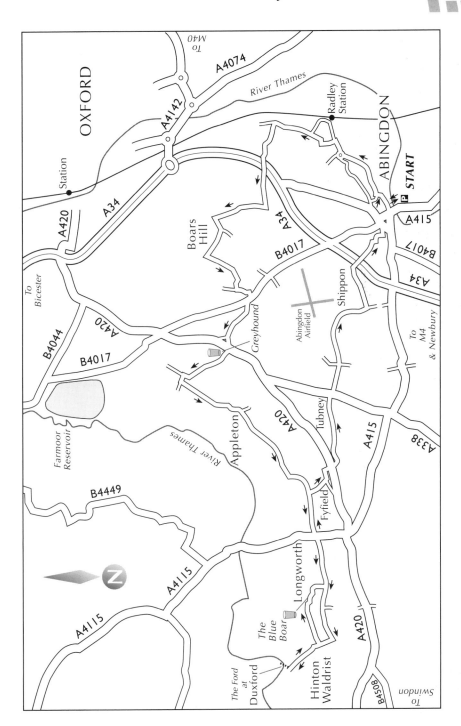

Appleton. The Thames is now below and to your right. Continue through Appleton. Cross the A415 and continue through Longworth and into Hinton Waldrist. Take the second **turn R** in the village (signed Duxford).

Follow the road down the hill. Once it flattens out look for a farm on your right. Just after this you should see a small cluster of thatched cottages. Take the bridle track to your right in front of the cottages. This leads to the ford. Crossing the ford by bicycle is only possible during dry summers, and should only be done with care as its surface can be slippery with waterweed, and there are pot holes on the far side. When you are ready to continue, retrace your steps to as far as Hinton Waldrist church. **Turn L** and where the road bears sharp right take the bridle track which continues straight ahead (signed Longworth). You will emerge on a tarmac road beside Longworth Manor, a very handsome building with impressive looking stables. Keep straight on and **bear R** by the church. **Turn L** at the T-junction and continue through the village until you reach a further T-junction. **Turn L** (signed Appleton). Re-cross the A415 and then **turn R** (signed Fyfield).

Continue into the village and at the crossroads **turn L** (signed No Through Road, Village Only). If the gate is shut, push your bike around the side. **Turn R** (easy to miss!) to go under the A420. Once through the

underpass, **bear L**. **Turn R** onto Abingdon Road. At the junction with the A338 **turn R** and immediately **turn L** (signed Cothill). Continue on this road through Gozzards Ford. **Turn L** (signed Shippon).

Turn R and cross the A34 on a bridge. Go straight on at the first mini roundabout. Soon you will see the entrance to Albert Park on your right. Cross the road and push your bike through the posts. Continue straight ahead, with the memorial to Prince Albert directly ahead of you. **Turn L** at the T-junction. **Turn L** at the next T-junction (Park Road). The road ends at a barrier. Push through and cross the main road at the pedestrian lights. Keep straight on and proceed into Bath Street. **Turn L** at the Black Swan into a shopping precinct (no cycling!). **Turn R** and soon you will emerge in the Market Square with the imposing façade of the Old County Hall (now the museum) ahead of you. Cross over High Street (care!). To your left is Bridge Street which leads back to the car parks.

· ·

ABINGDON

The market town of Abingdon is the site of the oldest continually occupied settlement in England. Excavations show that it has been occupied for 6,000 years. Between 3,000 and 1,500 years ago it was the site of a ceremonial avenue or cursus which ran for 1½ miles and the surrounding area would have been marked by ceremonial stone monuments. Later its

Cycling across the Thames at Duxford

position led to it becoming first an important trading centre for the ancient Britons and then a Roman town. An abbey was founded here in the 7th century which later became one of the richest and largest Benedictine sites in the country. In medieval times the tension between the abbey and the townsfolk spilled over and the abbey was torched. It was finally dismantled during the dissolution.

For many years Abingdon was the county town of Berkshire and as such held assizes in the Old County Hall. This elegant building built around 1680 by Christopher Kempster still shelters the weekly market and houses the local museum. On important royal occasions it is the centre of a tradition, unique to Abingdon, that of bun throwing.

JARN MOUND

Jarn Mound, and much of the surrounding area, is now looked after by the Oxford Preservation Trust. Jarn Mound itself is an artificial mound that was built between 1929 and 1931. It was the brainchild of Sir Arthur Evans, the well-known archaeologist, who lived locally and wanted to ensure that a view of the 'dreaming spires' was preserved at a time when other viewpoints were threatened with development. He also oversaw the preservation of Matthew Arnold's Field so that the landscape which inspired the poet and appeared in *Thyrsis* and in *The Scholar Gypsy* would not be lost. Today, the whole area is criss-crossed with numerous paths and is a very pleasant place to wander around, or to rest after climbing the hill.

(10)

The Iron Age Thames: Dorchester and Wittenham Clumps

14 miles

This ride may be short on miles but it is high on interest. The starting point is Dorchester-on-Thames with its Iron Age earthworks, Roman and early Christian connections. The route begins an anti-clockwise loop passing over the river at Clifton Hampden before visiting Long Wittenham, home of the Pendon Museum. We continue to Little Wittenham and on to Wittenham Clumps, the site of an Iron Age hill fort, and a great place for picnicking and flying kites. We then return to Little Wittenham and cross the Thames at Day's Lock. The route then takes a bridle path to Dorchester alongside some linear earthworks.

Map: OS Landranger 164 Oxford, Chipping Norton and Bicester (GR 579939).

Starting point: The route starts from the bridge over the River Thames in Dorchester-on-Thames, about 10 miles south-east of Oxford. The nearest train station is Culham, some 4 miles to the west. There is a car park with public toilets just to the town side of the bridge.

Chester's Tea Rooms (Queen Street, Dorchester) is open all year for drinks and light meals. Teas are served in the abbey grounds on Sunday afternoons from 3 pm (Easter to September). Refreshments are also available at Notcutt's Garden Centre near the Golden Balls roundabout. If you prefer a pub lunch we recommend the Machine Man in Long Wittenham.

The route is almost entirely flat, the only hill being the optional climb from Little Wittenham to the picnic area at Wittenham Clumps. The ride includes about one mile of track from Day's Lock to Dorchester.

Turn **L** out of the car park and proceed down High Street through the centre of Dorchester. **Turn R** (Drayton Road, cul-de-sac). Cross the A4074 on the Queensford Bridge. The road descends and bends to the right. Before this happens, **turn L** onto a stony track (no signpost), descend to road level and **bear R** to ride parallel with the road for about 50 yards. **Turn R** through barriers onto a road with a lake on

The Sinodun Hills, a familiar landmark

your right. Continue to the T-junction and **turn R** (no signpost). Follow the road through Drayton St Leonard, bearing sharp right (signed Stadhampton). Continue to cross the River Thame and shortly after **turn L** at the T-junction (signed Stadhampton). In Stadhampton **turn L** at the T-junction (signed Chiselhampton). In Chiselhampton **turn L** (signed Clifton Hampden).

Follow this road for some 2½ miles till you reach the Golden Balls roundabout. Go straight over (signed Clifton Hampden). There are traffic lights at the T-junction with the A415. **Turn R** (signed Culham) and immediately **turn L** (signed Wittenhams/Didcot). Proceed through the village and cross the Thames.

If you want to visit the Pendon Museum (a 1 mile detour), **bear R** on entering Long Wittenham (signed Appleford) and **turn R** (No Through Road) by the war memorial. The museum is along this road to your right. Otherwise on entering Long Wittenham **turn L** (signed Little Wittenham).

Turn R at the T-junction (signed Brightwell) and climb up a hill. Some ½ mile outside the village there is a car park on the left with access to Wittenham Clumps. Why not leave your bike and follow the track to the top of the hill? From there you can look down on Day's Lock and Dorchester with its Iron Age linear earthworks in the foreground and the abbey in the background.

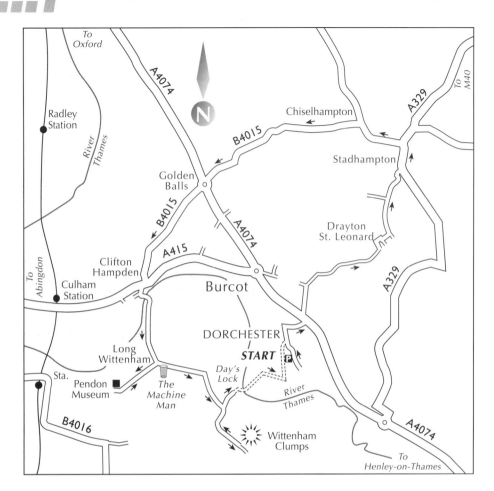

When you are ready, go back down the hill and into Little Wittenham. Keep straight on and freewheel down to Day's Lock. Cross the river on the bridge and go through the gate. Look ahead and to your left across the field you will see another gate. Cycle towards it across the field (this is a bridle path). Go through the second gate and follow the bridle track. Soon the track **bears R** running parallel with and to the left of a linear earthwork. This is a popular track for walkers, so take care. **Turn L** between two unfenced fields (no signpost) in the direction of some houses. **Turn R** (just before the houses start on both sides of the track) to follow the bridle track (no signpost) to meet the tarmac road. **Turn L** and follow the road till it meets the High Street. **Turn R** to return to the car park.

Long Wittenham – is this a real house or is it a model?

DORCHESTER-ON-THAMES

If you stand on Wittenham Clumps and look over the Thames to nearby Dorchester you cannot help but realise that you are looking down upon an area inhabited by man for thousands of years. You will see the linear earthwork (Dyke Hills) which separates Dorchester from the river. Beyond you will see the town, dominated by the abbey church of St Peter and St Paul.

Dorchester has been an important Christian centre since the missionary bishop Birinus (later saint) baptised Cynegils, pagan King of Wessex, here in AD 635. The present abbey church is thought to have been built on the site of the original Saxon abbey. It once held the shrine to St Birinus and was an important place of pilgrimage in the 13th and 14th centuries.

PENDON MUSEUM, LONG WITTENHAM

In the Pendon Museum, rural England of the 1930s and 1940s is captured in amazing detail in a series of large models. Several concentrate on the railways of the period. However, for me the most impressive is the Vale of the White Horse landscape which takes up most of the upper floor. The museum is open on Saturdays, Sundays and Bank Holiday Mondays (2 pm to 5 pm) for most of the year.

WITTENHAM CLUMPS

The two hills forming Wittenham Clumps (or the Sinodun Hills as they are also known) are a well-loved landmark in this part of Oxfordshire. Nowadays they are a popular location for picnics, walks and model aircraft flying.

(11)

Looking down from the Ridgeway

22 miles

This ride offers the rider the opportunity to look down on the Thames Valley from the Ridgeway, the ancient trackway running across the Berkshire Downs. From Didcot the route goes on road through Harwell village before climbing steadily to the Ridgeway using good quality bridle tracks. After riding a short section of the Ridgeway itself the route descends on road to East Hendred, a lovely village full of thatched cottages. The descent into the valley is complete by Steventon where the route uses the Priors' Causeway, part of a medieval raised cobbled track to Milton, where road is resumed. At Sutton Courtenay the route encounters the Thames. The return to Didcot uses a section of the National Cycle Route (No 5, London-Oxford).

Map: OS Landranger 174 Newbury and Wantage (GR 525905).

Starting point: This ride starts from Didcot railway station. Didcot lies on the London (Paddington) to Swindon and Bristol line. By car, Didcot is located close to the A34, some 14 miles south of Oxford. There is a car park adjacent to the station.

Food is available at Chilton Garden Centre, and at pubs such as the Wheatsheaf in East Hendred and the Swan or the George and Dragon in Sutton Courtenay. If the weather is fine, there is nothing better than a picnic on the Ridgeway or by the Thames at Sutton Pools.

This ride involves some climbing between Didcot and the Ridgeway, much of which is on bridle tracks. The tracks have a good surface and give expansive views of the surrounding countryside.

Turn R out of the station. **Turn L** at the roundabout (Foxhall Road, B4493) and **turn R** at the next roundabout (signed Harwell). Ride into the village of Harwell. **Turn L** (Church Lane) and **bear R** by the church entrance. **Turn R** (no signpost) and **turn L** (The Broadway, No Through Road). Push your bike up the ramp and carefully cross the Reading road (A417) onto the byway opposite (Holloway). Follow this track up the hill. Keep straight on at the crossroads with a second track. Pass underneath the A34 and emerge in Chilton village.

Turn R at the junction with the

The Thames at Sutton Pools, Sutton Courtenay

road. **Turn R** at the roundabout (signed Didcot/Wantage, A4185) and then **turn L** (signed Chilton School). Chilton Garden Centre is on your left. After passing the Horse and Jockey pub **turn R** onto a byway (signed Ridgeway) and follow this track till it meets the Ridgeway.

Initially the climb is gentle, but you may find it necessary to walk the last stretch. However, you will be well rewarded for your efforts as the view is expansive. Immediately below you are the buildings of the UKAE and the Rutherford-Appleton Laboratories. The latter includes the ISIS neutron source used by scientists worldwide to study the structure of materials. Ahead and to your left are Wantage and the Vale of the White Horse, and ahead and away to your right is the Thames Valley with the easily recognisable Wittenham Clumps.

Turn R and follow the Ridgeway for ½ mile, till it meets a road. **Turn R** onto the road and descend into East Hendred. Continue to the T-junction with the A417. **Turn R** (signed Reading) and soon **turn L** (signed Steventon, Heatherbed Lane). **Turn L** at the T-junction (no signpost) and at the traffic lights **turn L** (signed Steventon) and proceed down the hill and into Steventon.

Turn R immediately before the village hall (Milton Lane, No

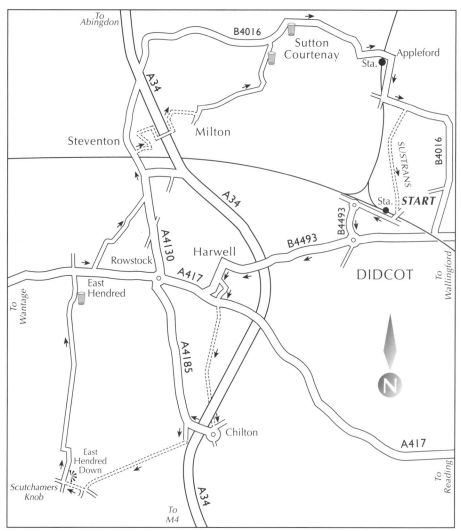

Through Road). **Bear R** and immediately **bear L** (signed Bridleway) onto the cobbled Priors' Causeway. Continue till you see the footbridge over the A34. **Bear R** and ride parallel to the road. **Turn L**, passing under the A34, and **turn L** again to reach the opposite side of the footbridge. Cross a small brook and **turn R**, following the brook.

After a while **bear R** and shortly emerge in Milton village.

Turn L onto the road and soon **turn R** (signed Sutton Courtenay). Keep straight on at the mini roundabout and **turn R** at the T-junction (signed Appleford). The abbey is to your right, and the path to Sutton Pools is a little further on your left as the

The Thames Valley from the Ridgeway

road bends right. Continue through Appleford, crossing the railway line.

Outside the village, where the road passes a level crossing on the right, **bear L**. Look out for a bridge over a brook, less than ½ mile further on. **Turn R** and follow the National Cycle Route 5 back into Didcot (take care not to miss a right hand turn at the crossroads of two tracks, signs on lamp posts). You will emerge near the bridge under the railway line. Go under the bridge and **turn R** onto Station Road to return to the station. If you have time, you could visit the Didcot Railway Centre nearby (see Route 12).

THE RIDGEWAY

The Ridgeway has been described as the 'greatest, lengthiest and noblest in appearance of all prehistoric roads'. It may well be among the oldest roads in the world. Today its status is byway not bridle path, reflecting its ancient usage. It runs along one of the six ridges that radiate from the Salisbury Plain, through Wiltshire, Oxfordshire and Berkshire. All along its length there is ample evidence of the prehistoric people who first trod it. There are earthworks aplenty, hill forts and the beautiful and ancient chalk hill figure, the Uffington White Horse. On the section covered in this ride, look out for Scutchamers Knob, just to the left of the Ridgeway, in the woods as you join the road to East Hendred. This dates from the Iron Age and at 77 ft high, it must have been an impressive site before 19th century archaeologists mutilated it. They found Iron Age pottery, an iron buckle and a charred oak post.

THE PRIORS' CAUSEWAY

This raised and cobbled causeway was built by the black monks of Steventon Priory for the purpose of improving access to the church in the wet season. The priory was a cell of the Abbey of Bec in Normandy. Some of the original medieval cobbles may still be seen, and indeed felt, as you ride along. Nowadays the causeway links Steventon with Milton. However, it is believed that it may originally have continued to Sutton Courtenay.

SUTTON COURTENAY

Sutton Courtenay is a pleasant village with the older houses arranged around a village green. At one end of the green is the abbey. This dates from around 1350. It was built on land owned by the powerful Abingdon Abbey and it may have been a summer residence for the Abbot or possibly it housed a monks' infirmary. In the churchyard are the graves of Herbert Henry Asquith, Prime Minister from 1908–1916, and Eric Blair, better known as the author George Orwell.

Sutton Pools lie just to the north of the village. Here the river descends over a series of weirs into the pools. Before the new Cut and Culham Lock were opened in 1809 there was a mill and pound lock at the pools. Because the lock took water from the mill to operate it, the miller exacted the single largest toll on the Thames, the considerable sum of 30 shillings per sixty tons in 1774.

12

The Iron Age and the Steam Age!

16 miles

This ride is a gentle exploration of some of the pretty villages sandwiched between the River Thames and the Berkshire Downs. The circuit begins by passing through North Moreton where some fine early stained glass can be seen in the church. It continues through South Moreton and on to the villages of Aston Tirrold and Aston Upthorpe. A bridleway then leads around the edge of the Iron Age hill fort on Blewburton Hill and on to Blewbury. We return to Didcot via the picture postcard village of East Hagbourne.

As you ride there is the opportunity for intimate glimpses of some of the best of rural architecture; black and white thatched cottages, decorative brickwork and flint. In the summer, the cottages and houses along the route display a rich variety of country gardens which add to the enjoyment and indeed fragrance of the ride.

Map: OS Landranger 174 Newbury and Wantage (GR 525905).

Starting point: This ride starts from Didcot railway station. Didcot lies on the London (Paddington) to Swindon and Bristol line. By car, Didcot is located close to the A34, some 14 miles south of Oxford. There is a car park adjacent to the station.

If you wish to have a meal along the route, the Crown at South Moreton and the Red Lion in Blewbury are recommended. However, on a fine day, leave your bike and walk up to the Iron Age fort on Blewburton Hill for a picnic and wonderful views of the Downs and the Thames Valley. The ride is not a long one, so there should be plenty of time for railway enthusiasts to satisfy their curiosity at the Didcot Railway Centre on their return.

The ride is gently undulating.

Turn L out of the station, along Station Road. **Turn L** and pass under the railway line (Cow Lane). Almost immediately ahead and to the left is a cycle track (signed Route 5 National Cycle Route). Follow the Route 5 signs, turning left along the line of some pylons. After a mile or so, the track enters a short tunnel under a road. Continue straight on with a brook to your left till you meet a road. **Turn R** onto the road (no signpost, you leave Route 5 at this point) and continue for about a

The impressive 13th century stained glass at All Saints' church, North Moreton

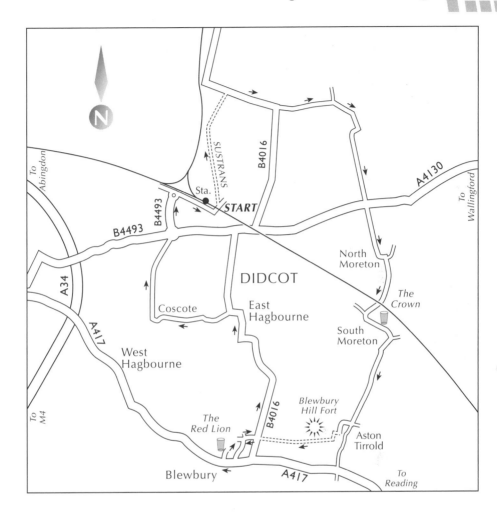

mile. **Turn R** (care!) on a sharp left hand bend (signed Brightwell/North Moreton) and climb the hill.

Turn R at the top (signed North Moreton). Go straight on at the crossroads with the A4130 (signed North Moreton). Follow the road into the village and continue as far as the church. On leaving the church retrace your steps for a short distance. **Turn L** (signed South

Moreton) and follow the road through South Moreton. **Bear R** (signed Aston Tirrold).

At the staggered crossroads in the village, turn right into Thorpe Street. **Turn L** and **turn R** onto a stone track immediately before the church. Follow the track up and around to the right between wooden farm buildings. **Turn R** onto an earth track where another track crosses (there is a partly hidden bridleway sign to your left) to run parallel with the line of Blewburton Hill. This track may be muddy after heavy rain. Halfway along is a stile, if you want to walk to the top. After ½ mile the stone track begins again and you will emerge in Blewbury.

Blewbury is full of elegant cottages and delightful nooks and crannies. For a tour of Blewbury, go straight on (Bessels Lea) then **turn L** (South Street). At the T-junction **turn R** onto the main road for a short stretch. **Turn R** (Nottingham Fee, No Through Road). **Bear R** by the Red Lion and proceed to the footpath barriers. **Turn L** and push your bike past Cleve Cottage and through the second barrier. **Turn R** (Church End) and **turn L** (South Street). **Turn R** (Bessels Lea) and return to the crossroads with the bridle track. **Turn L** (no signpost) onto the road. Otherwise **turn R** at the end of the bridle track to miss out Blewbury.

Proceed into East Hagbourne. On the outskirts, **turn L** (signed West Hagbourne). Follow the road through the village centre and **turn R** at the T-junction (signed Didcot). Keep on this road and cross straight over four mini roundabouts. Go straight on at the roundabout (signed Station, car park ½ mile). **Turn R** at the next roundabout onto Station Road and return to the start.

DIDCOT AND THE GREAT WESTERN RAILWAY

Unlike its close neighbour Abingdon, Didcot does not have a long and proud history. Instead, it owes its current existence to the coming of the railways, and in particular to Isambard Kingdom Brunel's Great Western Railway from London to Bristol (which incidentally Abingdon spurned). It is therefore fitting that Didcot is the location of the Great Western Collection containing steam locomotives, passenger carriages and freight wagons from the golden age of the steam railway along with numerous smaller items. The centre may be accessed from the station, and is open on Saturdays and Sundays throughout the year and daily throughout the summer and at other selected times. There is a refreshment room, picnic area and shop.

NORTH MORETON CHURCH

According to Pevsner, the stained glass in All Saints' church at North Moreton 'is probably the finest in Berkshire'; rare praise indeed and it is definitely worth a visit. Incidentally, since this was written, North Moreton has swapped allegiance to Oxfordshire. The window was endowed by Miles de Stapleton, a baron under Edward II, and was erected in 1299. In 1314 Miles was killed at the Battle of Bannockburn and the chapel held daily masses for the repose of his soul until the Reformation. The window consists of five lancets beneath an elaborate tracery. Each lancet contains three scenes and together the windows acted as an aid to devotion. They therefore give a unique insight into the important themes of 13th century theology.

13

William the Conqueror and Watercress

9 miles or 22 miles

This route offers a gentle exploration of villages to the east of Wallingford (Option 1). You will cross the Thames – by bridge, unlike William the Conqueror who forded the river here – and visit nearby Ewelme with its watercress beds. For the more adventurous, there is an longer route (Option 2) which involves a climb to and descent from the Chiltern escarpment. The ride climbs up the pleasant open valley of Swyncombe with its 12th century church at the top. It continues to Cookley Green before descending Howe Hill to Watlington. The route continues in flat country through one of the two Salomes in Oxfordshire (Berrick) to rejoin Option 1 at Benson. Whichever option you choose you will find pleasant riding awaiting you.

Map: Option 1 requires only the OS Landranger 175 Reading and Windsor; Option 2 also requires 164 Oxford, Chipping Norton and Bicester (GR 607895).

Starting point: The routes start from Wallingford on the River Thames, 10 miles south of Oxford and 16 miles north-west of Reading. The nearest railway stations are Didcot or Appleford (both about 6 miles away). There is a convenient car park (pay and display) on Castle Street, 100 yards from the start of this ride which is the crossroads in the centre of the town.

Wallingford has plenty of pubs for refreshments. In the summer there is a regular refreshment kiosk in the park by the bridge. The Lamb at Chalgrove and the Riverside Café at Benson are popular venues with local cyclists.

The basic route is flat and quite short. The longer route involves a climb into the Chilterns before continuing in a flatter landscape.

Starting out from the crossroads in the town centre, head out in an easterly direction crossing the bridge over the River Thames. Go straight on at the roundabout and ride through Crowmarsh Gifford. At the next roundabout take the second exit (signed Ewelme).

Turn R and immediately **turn L**, then **turn L again**, following signs for Ewelme. Just before you descend into the village there is a splendid view of the church and the valley –

Wallingford Castle Gardens

do pause a while to admire it. After the descent (take care here) into the village there is a choice of route. **Turn L** and head through the village for Benson and back to Wallingford, or **turn R** for a longer ride and a climb into the edge of the Chiltern Hills.

Option 1 (9 miles)

Turn L and ride through Ewelme. There is a stream running alongside the road and in places there are watercress beds. At the road junction at the end of the village **bear sharp L** (signed Wallingford). Immediately after the bridge over the stream **bear sharp R** (signed Benson). The road passes along the edge of RAF Benson airfield, then into Benson village. At the end of High Street there is a series of bends and junctions. On a right hand bend **turn L** (signed Wallingford); the war memorial stands at this junction. (**Option 2** joins at this point.)

Pigs might fly, at least in Chalgrove

At the T-junction (A4074) you have a choice. If you want to visit the Riverside Café and shop, **turn R** (for safety use the footpath and traffic island to cross as this road can be very busy at times) and a few yards along the main road **turn L**. Upon leaving, push your bicycle and **turn R** out of the Riverside Café, staying on the same side of the road and continuing into the start of the road leading to Preston Crowmarsh. If you are not visting the café, **turn L** at the T-junction and immediately **turn R** (signed Preston Crowmarsh). Ride through Preston Crowmarsh. At the T-junction with the A4074 **turn R** to join the footpath/cycle track. After a short distance the pathway veers to the right following the path of the old road out of

Wallingford, now a quiet backwater (no entry for motor vehicles). On the right is the Wallingford Hydraulic Research Centre. The road ends at the first roundabout you met on the way out of Wallingford. Here **turn R** to head back into Wallingford town centre.

Option 2 (22 miles)
Turn R when you reach Ewelme (signed Swyncombe). After a short distance **turn L** (signed Swyncombe). The Ridgeway crosses this road near the top of the hill. The 12th century church is well-signed, being located at the end of a track off to the right of the road. After the climb to Swyncombe carry on to Cookley Green. In the village **turn L** onto the B481 (signed

Watlington). Just after the sign for Britwell Salome on the left, there is a steep descent known as Howe Hill – take care here. As the road levels out the hill to your right is known as Watlington Hill. Soon you will enter Watlington itself.

A quick tour of Watlington may be had by **turning R** into Couching Street (signed Chinnor). **Take the first L** into High Street and **turn L again** at the end of the street into Gorwell. **Turn R** (signed Oxford) at the T-junction (Brook Street) and very soon **turn R again** (signed Oxford) joining the B480. Stay on the B480 through the village of Cuxham. Follow the road to the right (signed Stadhampton).

Turn L into Chalgrove (signed Chalgrove) and **turn R** into High Street. At this point you may wish to **turn L** (Church Lane) to investigate the church which contains some unusual medieval wall paintings. Otherwise ride down High Street and **turn L** (signed Ewelme, Mill Lane). The Lamb public house stands on the right hand side of this junction.

Turn R at the T-junction (signed Berrick Salome). At the edge of Berrick Salome **bear L** at the fork. In the village **bear R** (signed Benson). Ride through Rokemarsh then **turn R** at the crossroads onto the B4009 (signed Benson). In Benson follow the road to the T-junction then **turn R** then almost immediately **turn L** (signed Wallingford). The war

memorial stands on the junction. Rejoin Option 1 and continue back to Wallingford.

WALLINGFORD

Wallingford originated as a fortified Saxon town or burgh. William the Conqueror forded the Thames here after the Battle of Hastings and the motte and bailey castle was one of the first to be built after the invasion, in 1071. Wallingford was a staunch Royalist stronghold in the Civil War which explains why Oliver Cromwell ordered the castle to be destroyed. All that remains now are a few walls and some impressive earthworks which form part of the wonderfully tranquil Castle Gardens whose entrance is next to the Castle Street car park.

EWELME

Ewelme is a pleasant brick and flint village. Its name means 'spring' or 'source of water' and it's not difficult to understand why, as a crystal clear stream flows through the village, feeding watercress beds. The current beds were built around 1925 and were in commercial operation until 1965. Take some time to explore the scenic church and adjoining medieval school and almshouses. This was a classic combination of buildings which rarely survives to the modern day intact. Indeed the school here is still in use. Ewelme's institutions were founded by Alice Chaucer, granddaughter of the poet and wife of the Duke of Suffolk. The churchyard contains the grave of Jerome K. Jerome whose tale *Three Men in a Boat* still epitomises for many leisure time on the Thames.

14

Around the Goring Gap

23 miles

One of the most important outcrops of rocks in southern Britain is the chalk escarpment running from Wiltshire in the west to Bedfordshire in the east. This was laid down more than 100 million ago when the whole area lay underneath a shallow warm sea. The River Thames cuts through this escarpment at the Goring Gap. To the east of the gap are the Chiltern Hills, and to the west the Berkshire Downs. This ride investigates both sides of the gap, initially climbing up into the Chiltern side and descending to cross the Thames at Whitchurch before climbing once again, this time into the Berkshire Downs.

The rural architecture on either side of the gap is similar and dominated by flint and brick. As you will see, the Chilterns are more heavily wooded, while the Berkshire Downs have a more open feel to them and agriculture is more important. It is always interesting to see how a physical barrier such as a river can give rise to quite different land use and character on either side.

Map: OS Landranger 174 Newbury and Wantage and 175 Reading and Windsor (GR 603806).

Starting point: This ride starts from the railway station in Goring, some 8 miles north-west of Reading. The town lies on the line from Paddington to Bristol. If you arrive by car, there is a car park on Station Road which runs parallel to and to the east of High Street.

There are several pubs serving food around the route. We recommend the Catherine Wheel in Goring (Station Road) and the White Hart in Hampstead Norreys. There is also The Riverside Café, by the bridge in Goring, and a coffee shop at the Wyld Court Rainforest Centre, near Hampstead Norreys.

The ride is a challenging one with several climbs. However, if you climb at your own pace, you will be rewarded with views back into the Goring Gap and the quiet countryside around.

Turn **L** out of Goring station then **turn R** by the Queen's Arms pub. In Cray's Pond **turn R** (signed Whitchurch/Pangbourne). Follow the road through Whitchurch Hill. Cross the toll bridge (free to cyclists)

The Aldworth Giants in St Mary's church, Aldworth

and ride into Pangbourne.

In the centre of Pangbourne **turn R** then **turn L** at the mini roundabouts, (signed A340, Basingstoke). **Turn R** near the church (signed Upper Basildon). Climb the hill and stay on the same road for about 3½ miles. **Turn R** at the T-junction (signed Yattendon). Continue through Yattendon. **Turn R** at the Royal Oak (signed Hampstead Norreys) and at the T-junction, **turn R** again (signed Hampstead Norreys).

At the edge of Hampstead Norreys **turn L** to join the B4009. By turning right at this junction you can visit the Wyld Court Rainforest Centre (a detour of about 1½ miles).

Ride into the centre of Hampstead Norreys. **Turn R** at the mini roundabout (signed Compton), then at the T-junction, **turn R again** (signed Compton). **Turn R** (signed Hackney Bottom). At the T-junction **turn R** (signed Streatley).

Turn L at the staggered crossroads, also known as 'Four Points' (signed B4009, Aldworth). In Aldworth **turn L** to visit the church and the Aldworth Giants contained therein. After visiting the church go back to the B4009 and **turn L**. At the crossroads **turn R** (signed Upper Basildon). **Turn L** at the fork (signed Southridge). **Keep L** at the grass triangle with Southridge Farm and house on the left. **Keep L again**, shortly passing by Manor Farm on

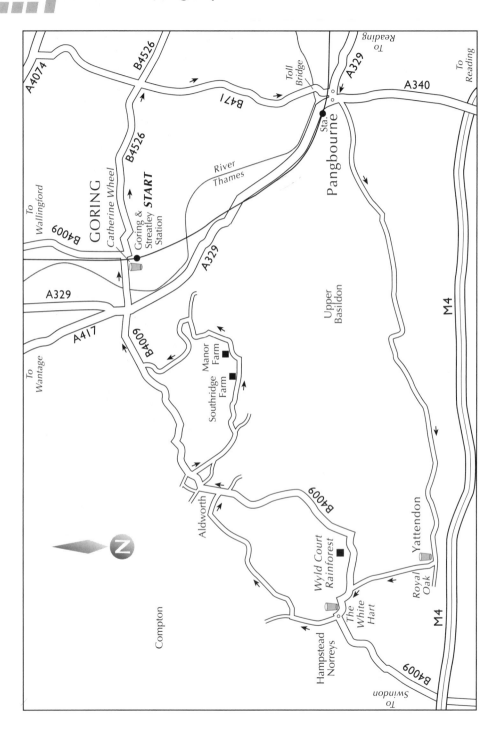

the left hand side of the road.

Soon after passing Manor Farm there is a steep and twisting descent (care, gravel and stones on road) leading to a T-junction. **Turn L** (sharp) (signed Aldworth) at this T-junction. Follow the road until the T-junction with the B4009 where you **turn R** (no signpost). Soon there is a steep descent ending with crossroads and traffic lights (care!).

At the crossroads go straight across and ride into Streatley and Goring. To return to the railway station, stay on the main road (High Street), cross the railway line on the bridge, and **turn R** at the T-junction. Follow signs to the station.

THE WYLD COURT RAINFOREST CENTRE

The rainforest centre is a short detour (less than 1½ miles) from the route on the B4009 to the east of Hampstead Norreys. It is open all year (except Christmas and Boxing Days). In its large glasshouses, the correct conditions are maintained by a sophisticated computer-controlled system of ventilators, thermal screens and sprinklers to mimic three different rain forest climates: Lowland Tropical, Amazonica and Cloud Forest. It's a fascinating collection that has been built up with a great deal of skill and much enthusiasm. In the summer and autumn you can see the giant water lily *Victoria Amazonica*, whose leaves can grow to more than 8 ft in diameter. However, visit the centre on a winter ride and you will be transported from greyness and cold into a wonderfully warm riot of colour and smell, the highlight of which is the many exotic flowering orchids.

THE ALDWORTH GIANTS

Enter the church of St Mary in the tiny village of Aldworth and you are in for a surprise, for within are huge sculptures of nine members and three generations of the de la Beche family. Larger than life and dressed in their finery they lie in the nave, six of them under elaborately carved stone canopies. The family originated in Flanders and as supporters of William of Normandy came over here in the early years after the Conquest. They built a castle at Aldworth and were granted the land encompassing several of the surrounding villages. By the end of the 13th century they had made significant social strides and several generations held posts at court. The figures are thought to have been placed here in the mid 14th century shortly before the family became extinct in the male line, thus recording for posterity the family in its heyday.

15

Goring, the Ridgeway and Lord Nuffield's Place

30 miles

This ride starts by leaving Goring along the famed Ridgeway beside the River Thames to South Stoke. It then takes to the road to North Stoke before heading east to visit Nuffield, the home of Lord Nuffield (formerly William Morris of car fame). The ride uses a delightful bridle track to skirt the edge of Stoke Row. It then passes the Well Place Zoo with its collection of birds from around the world before returning to Goring over open arable land giving excellent views of the Goring Gap.

Map: OS Landranger 175 Reading and Windsor (a tiny fraction of the route is on 174 Newbury and Wantage, but you can do without it) (GR 603806).

Starting point: This ride starts from the railway station in Goring, some 8 miles north-west of Reading. The town lies on the line from Paddington to Bristol. If you arrive by car, there is a car park on Station Road which runs parallel to and to the east of High Street.

There are several pubs serving food around the route. We recommend the Catherine Wheel in Goring (Station Road) and the Cherry Tree in Stoke Row. There is also The Riverside Café, by the bridge in Goring.

The ride is the longest in the book and it makes a fine day out, especially if you take the opportunity to visit the places of interest en route.

Starting from the railway station **turn L** onto the B4009. After a short distance **turn L** (signed Newbury/Streatley). Soon after passing the sign for the car park on your right, **turn R** into Cleeve Road. This road joins the Ridgeway. At the junction go straight on to stay on Cleeve Road. Keep straight on, following signs for the Ridgeway (marked as a bridle path). After riding along the Ridgeway, with the River Thames below and to your left you will come to a 'Private Road' sign. Keep straight on here as the bridle path and the Ridgeway run along the path of the road. The path soon becomes a gravel path, then a dirt path. At the end of the dirt path section you arrive in South Stoke.

Goring Lock

Nuffield Place, home of Lord Nuffield

Soon after passing the church on your right **turn R** (no signpost). At the crossroads with the B4009 **turn L** (signed Crowmarsh/Wallingford). Ride along the B4009 to North Stoke where you **turn R** (signed Stoke Row/Well Place Zoo).

Go straight on at the staggered crossroads with the A4074 (signed Ipsden). **Turn L** at the crossroads (signed Hailey/Crowmarsh). **Turn R** (no signpost, but 3 ton weight limit sign at the start of the road). **Turn R** at the crossroads (no sign, but within sight of main A4130 road). Ride into Nuffield. If you wish to visit Nuffield Place, it is located on the other side of the A4130, so **turn L** and at the A4130 **turn L** and almost immediately **turn R**. The

entrance to Nuffield Place is a short way along to your right. Otherwise **turn R** at the T-junction (signed Stoke Row). **Turn L** (Whitcalls Lane). Soon after passing Oakingham House (on the right) **bear L** to join a narrow grassy path. The path, which can get a little overgrown at times, becomes wider at the bottom of the slope in woodland. It widens again to become a small lane. At the T-junction **turn R**. **Turn R** at the crossroads (signed Stoke Row). In Stoke Row **turn L** (signed Peppard).

Turn R at the crossroads (signed Hook End). At the following crossroads **turn R** (no signpost, but look to your left and you will a sign marking the Sustrans National

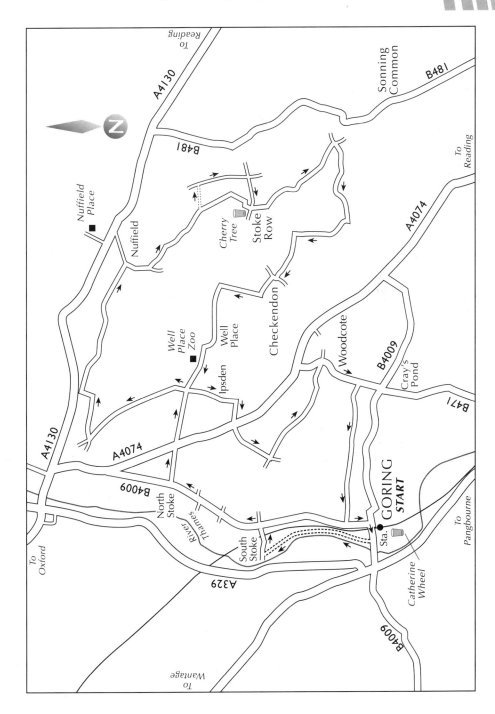

Cycle Network Route 5. **Turn L** (no signpost, but Sustrans Route No 5 sign on the junction) leaving the national route. Ride into Checkendon.

In Checkendon **turn R** at the T-junction (no signpost). Soon **turn L** (signed Ipsden). **Turn R** (signed Ipsden). At the crossroads where Scot's Common and Three Corner Common meet **turn L** (signed Ipsden). Ignore the left turning to Ipsden and carry on to the T-junction where you **turn L** (signed Well Place). This section of the road starts fairly flat followed by a steep twisting descent (CARE!). There is a sharp left hand bend at the bottom of the descent and there is often loose gravel. Just after the sharp bend the Well Place Zoo is on the right. If not visiting the zoo carry on to the crossroads where you **turn L** (signed Ipsden/Woodcote). (**Turn R** out of the zoo to reach the crossroads.)

Keep straight on through the village and go straight on at the crossroads (signed Woodcote/Braziers Park). **Turn R** (signed Woodcote/Goring). At the crossroads with the A4074 go straight on (signed South Stoke/Goring). **Turn L** at the crossroads (signed Woodcote). In Woodcote **turn R** (signed Goring/Whitchurch). Ride out of the village then soon **turn R** at the crossroads (signed Cleeve, Shivell's Hill to the left). Keep straight on until the crossroads (in the part of Goring known as Cleeve) with the B4009 where you **turn L** then go straight on again and back to the railway station.

NUFFIELD PLACE

For 30 years from 1933–1963 Nuffield Place was the home of William Morris, later Lord Nuffield, the founder of Morris Motors of Cowley, Oxford. Although he is best remembered as an industrialist he also left his mark as a philanthropist, giving away around £30 million in his own lifetime. Nuffield Place is not an old house, being built in 1912. Its lack of pretension and its contents, which are all of high quality without being unduly flashy, project an image of a complex man who cared deeply about his own community. Nuffield Place is open on the second and fourth Sundays of each month between May and September from 2 pm to 5 pm. Veteran cars are often on display.

IPSDEN

From the secluded village of Ipsden a series of valleys run up into the Chiltern Hills. The village was founded along with the church around the year 1200. At this time thick woods covered the area and the village settlers would have had to hack the woodland back to clear enough room for dwellings and typically two or possibly three large fields which would have been strip farmed.

Ipsden church possesses some interesting double-sided brasses or palimpsests and the 300 plus foot deep well sunk into the chalk of the churchyard illustrates one of the abiding problems of living in this area, that of getting water.

(16)

Kenneth Grahame's Thames

21 miles

This route has some rather steep hills as it climbs out of the valley and into part of the Chiltern Hills area. The ride has a strong *Wind in the Willows* connection. The Berkshire Thames of Kenneth Grahame's childhood provides the setting of the book and Mapledurham House (which can be visited as part of this ride) is believed to have been the model for Toad Hall. Grahame spent his last few years living at Pangbourne. There is also an opportunity along the route to investigate one of the Chilterns' more bizarre sights, the Maharajah's Well at Stoke Row.

In spring, the woods are alive with more shades of green than you can imagine, in the summer the leafy lanes and dappled sunlight are a delight, in the autumn the countryside is awash with brown and gold and the air pungent with the aroma of wild mushrooms and in the winter the views open, and the hills and river can be seen more clearly.

Map: OS Landranger 175 Reading and Windsor (GR 632766).

Starting point: The ride starts from the railway station in Pangbourne, 6 miles west of Reading. Pangbourne is on the railway line between Paddington and Didcot and Oxford. Thames Trains provide a regular service on which bicycles may be carried free. Car parking is available at the railway station.

The Cherry Tree at Stoke Row is a good refreshment stop or why not take a picnic and enjoy it at the Riverside Park in Mapledurham?

The roads used are, as far as possible, quiet narrow leafy lanes. However, some lanes have potholes, and gravel may be washed out onto the road which can be hazardous, especially on bends and at the bottom of hills. Providing care is exercised these roads are a delight to ride along and the effort of the climbs brings a rich reward.

Leave Pangbourne railway station and **turn R**. After a short distance **turn L** at the mini roundabout (signed Reading, A329). **Turn L** **again** at the next mini roundabout (signed Whitchurch, B471). After crossing the toll bridge (free for cyclists) into Whitchurch on

Relaxing on the bank of the Thames at Mapledurham

Thames, the B471, **take the second turn R** (Hardwick Road). After leaving the houses behind you and at gates, the road bears left and starts to climb sharply. Follow the road to the crossroads at Goring Heath (Goring Heath post office stands on the right hand side at this junction). **Turn R** (signed Mapledurham).

To visit the watermill, house and riverside picnic area at Mapledurham **turn R**, following the brown signposts. After the visit to Mapledurham retrace your path to rejoin the Goring Heath road, where you **turn R**. If you are not interested in the visit, then carry straight on.

At the T-junction with the A4074 **turn L** (signed Oxford) and soon **turn R** (signed Tokers Green). Take care, as the junction is on a curve in the road which can be very busy at times. In the village **turn L** at the T-junction for Kidmore End. **Turn R** and immediately **turn L** (signed Sonning Common).

In Sonning Common keep straight on until a double T-junction. Here **turn R** and immediately **turn L** to join the B481 (signed Peppard). At the next crossroads **turn L** (signed Nettlebed, B481). **Bear R** at the fork, following signs for Nettlebed/ Watlington (B481).

Stay on the B481 until you get to Highmoor Crosss (signed

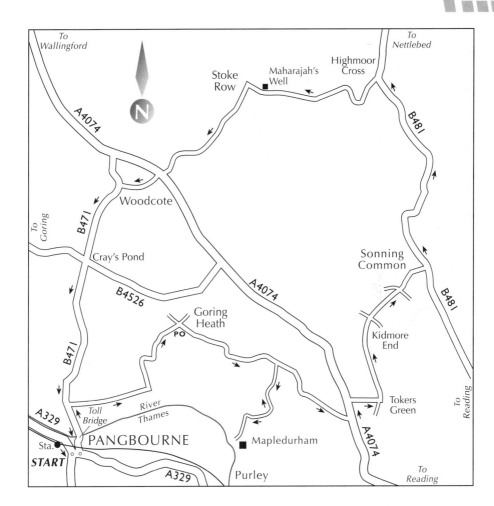

Highmoor). **Turn L** (signed Stoke Row). Descend (with care – loose gravel and potholes at the bottom of the hill) then climb to Stoke Row village. The Maharajah's Well is on the right hand side of the road.

Turn L (signed Checkendon, Uxmore Road). Ride through Checkendon and keep straight on until you get to the junction with the A4074. Here **turn R and**

immediately **turn L**, following signs to Woodcote. In Woodcote **turn L** (signed Goring/Whitchurch, B471). In Cray's Pond follow the signs for Whitchurch). Stay on the B471 through Whitchurch Hill and Whitchurch on Thames (signed Whitchurch Hill) and on to Pangbourne where you retrace your path back to the railway station, by **turning R** at each mini roundabout.

MAPLEDURHAM

Mapledurham House is one of the finest Tudor houses in Oxfordshire. It was built by Sir Richard Blount, beginning in 1585, in red brick with local flint dressing. The Blounts are a Catholic family and during the periods of persecution had a priest hole, trap door and secret passages built into the house. The house was fortified during the Civil War. Nearby, on the banks of the Thames and part of the Thames Riverside Picnic Park, is a weatherboarded 15th century watermill, a rare example of a working Thames watermill. The wooden machinery is powered by an undershot waterwheel and wholemeal flour is still ground and sold on site. Both the house and mill are regularly open to the public.

MAHARAJAH'S WELL, STOKE ROW

The Maharajah's Well with its oriental design, bright colours and gold elephant must have seemed even more incongruous when it was completed in 1864 than it does today. It was built thanks to a gift of money by the Maharajah of Benares (in India) to mark his respect for all things British (especially the Royal Family) and for the fifth son of the Squire of nearby Ipsden, Mr Charles Reade, who had aided him for a number of years. The Maharajah chose to build a well after recalling a conversation he had had with Mr Reade around 1850 about the problems the local villagers had obtaining adequate supplies of water in what was then a remote and high part of the Chilterns. The well is an impressive feat of engineering. First a hole 368 ft (deeper than St Paul's Cathedral is high!) by 4 ft wide was dug by hand before being lined with bricks. From the bottom the sky must be a mere pinprick of light! In its heyday the well provided 600–700 gallons of water daily.

17

Henley, Russell's Water and Nettlebed: Red Kite Country

19 miles

This ride explores the countryside to the north and west of Henley. The route begins by riding through the small village of Bix, before descending into Bix Bottom. A climb, part on and part off road through a pleasant wood, brings you out at Maidensgrove and Russell's Water Common, a popular picnic destination. Look out, and perhaps you will see some of the impressive red kites which were introduced to the area a decade ago and have now settled in so well. With their 4 ft wing span and forked tail they are a beautiful and unmistakable sight.

The ride returns through Nettlebed, where you can see the bottle-shaped brick kiln, and then continues through quiet leafy lanes to Henley. A short detour offers the opportunity of visiting Greys Court owned by the National Trust.

Map: OS Landranger 175 Reading and Windsor (GR 764826).

Starting point: The route starts from the stone bridge over the Thames at Henley which is about 7 miles north-east of Reading or 9 miles west of Maidenhead. It is accessible by train from London (Paddington), Reading and Twyford. If arriving by car, there is ample parking with toilets and a nearby café at Mill Meadows (follow signs in Henley for long term parking) which is at the end of Meadow Road, just behind the railway station.

There is a huge selection of cafés, restaurants and pubs in Henley. A convenient pub along the route is the Dog and Duck in Highmoor, whose portions live up to their description of 'generous'! Light refreshments are also available at Greys Court when open. Otherwise, if the weather is fine, Russell's Water Common is a lovely spot for a picnic.

This is a lovely ride, albeit hilly.

From the bridge, head off in a westerly direction, that is, into town (signed Wallingford, A4130). At the crossroads with traffic lights go straight on (signed Peppard) and uphill. Ride on for about 2 miles then **turn R** on a left hand bend (signed Bix). Follow the signs for Bix. Ride through Broadplat (no name sign) then on to the

A quiet road in the Chilterns

crossroads with the A4130. Go straight on and ride into Bix village. Ride through the village, passing the church on the right hand side of the road. **Turn L** into Rectory Lane (signed Oxfordshire Cycleway). After a steep descent (care!) **turn L** at the T-junction (signed Oxfordshire Cycleway).

After a gentle climb **turn R** onto a track (signed Oxfordshire Way). The continuing climb on this track is quite steep in places, but it can be ridden all of the way! Otherwise dismount and enjoy walking through a pleasant woodland nature reserve. As the track joins a small road (no signpost) **bear L** to head for Maidensgrove. At the T-junction **turn L** (climbing left) and

within 50 yards you will emerge on Russell's Water Common.

Ride through the village of Russell's Water and then on to the T-junction with the B481. **Turn L** at the T-junction (signed Nettlebed). Ride through the village of Cookley Green and stay on the B481 until you reach Nettlebed. In Nettlebed **turn L** onto the A4130 noting the bottle kiln on the left, then **turn R** at the roundabout (signed B481, Reading/Peppard). Stay on the B481 and ride through the village of Highmoor.

When you arrive at the start of the village called Satwell, a short distance after Highmoor, **turn left** (signed Shepherd's Green). **Turn L**

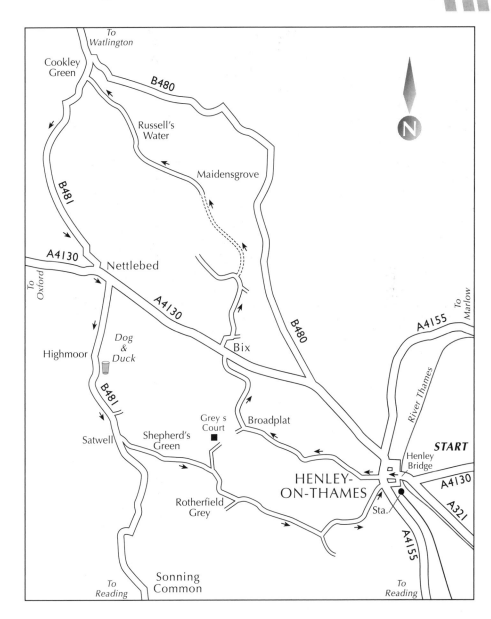

at the junction (signed Greys). The Lamb Inn is nearby. Just after Shepherd's Green **bear L** at the fork for Greys. In the village **bear L** following signs for Greys Court. (If you don't want to go to Greys Court then **turn R**, signed for Harpsden.) Otherwise from Greys Court **turn R** and continue to Rotherfield Greys. **Turn L** (no signpost) and soon **turn**

L again (no signpost).

Stay on this road which becomes Greys Road after rounding a left hand bend. Go straight on at the mini roundabout and straight on at the staggered crossroads with traffic lights. This brings you out by the River Thames and close to the bridge where the ride started.

● ●

NETTLEBED

An interesting feature in Nettlebed is the restored 300 year old brick kiln of bottle design. This is typical of kilns which were once part of many villages hereabouts. All the raw materials for brickmaking were available locally. The chalk deposits of the Chiltern escarpment are capped with a layer of clay, and there was plenty of wood to fuel the kilns. Several families in the village were active in this trade for many generations. The forerunners of this particular kiln produced the 35,000 tiles for Wallingford Castle, and in 1416 the cost of the 200,000 bricks bought to build Stonor House and made here was £40.

GREYS COURT

A picturesque 14th century house with later additions. The interior contains fine examples of 18th century plasterwork, and the outbuildings include a Tudor wheelhouse and pleasant walled garden. The house is open from April till the end of September on Wednesday, Thursday, Friday and Bank Holiday Mondays (closed Good Friday) 2 pm to 6 pm. The garden is open from April to September daily except Sunday and Monday (closed Good Friday but open on Bank Holiday Mondays) 2 pm to 6 pm.

18

Henley, Fingest and Hambleden

16½ miles

This ride explores both the woods and villages in the Chiltern valleys (or more correctly bottoms) to the north of Henley. The initial part of the ride involves some climbing, but you will be rewarded with expansive views of the Thames Valley and hills towards Cookham and Maidenhead, and then a scenic and gentle descent between the picturesque villages of Fingest and Hambleden. Although the route doesn't pass through the centre of these villages, you won't regret taking a few moments to explore them more fully. They are full of the flint and brick cottages so typical of the area.

The final section of the route crosses the Thames over the weir at Mill End and returns on a quiet road close to the river back to Henley along the section of Thames raced along during the famous regatta. It is always interesting watching the craft on the river – they can vary from humble rowing boats and small launches to huge polished monsters that would look more at home in St Tropez.

Map: OS Landranger 175 Reading and Windsor (GR 764826).

Starting point: The route starts from the stone bridge over the Thames at Henley which is 7 miles north-east of Reading or 9 miles west of Maidenhead. It is accessible by train from London (Paddington), Reading and Twyford. If arriving by car, there is ample parking with toilets and a nearby café at Mill Meadows (follow signs in Henley for long term parking) which is at the end of Meadow Road, just behind the railway station.

There is a huge selection of cafés, restaurants and pubs in Henley. Along the route there are several pubs – for example, the Chequers Inn at Fingest and the Frog at Skirmett.

The early part of the ride has several climbs but there is a lovely descent from Fingest down the dry valley to Hambleden. This route has a marvellous mixture of scenery.

From the bridge, head in a westerly direction – into the town (signed Wallingford, A4130). **Turn R** at the traffic lights (signed Oxford, A4130). **Turn R** at two mini roundabouts (signed Maidenhead, A4155).

The river at Henley

Just over a mile from the junction (and opposite the Toad Hall Garden Centre) **turn L** off the A4155 onto a small road (signed Fawley). **Turn R** at the T-junction (signed Fawley). Ride for just over ½ mile then **turn L** (signed Fawley Bottom); there is a church near the corner. Descend the steep hill (take care) to Fawley Bottom and **bear R** at the junction (no signpost). Stay on this road and then **turn L** (signed Southend). Ride through the edge of Southend (not 'on Sea'!) to Summer Heath. **Turn R** at the T-junction (signed Fingest). **Turn R** (no signpost) and ride into Fingest. If you are not interested in seeing anything in the village **turn R** (signed Skirmett).

In Skirmett stay on the 'major road' following signs for Hambleden. At Hambleden the 'main road' passes through the outer edge of the village, but a small road loops off to the left (signed Hambleden) into the heart of the village. Going around this loop is well worth it. By bearing right around the loop you rejoin the 'main road' to **turn L** and return to your original route. On Sundays in summertime, tea and cakes are available in the church.

The road comes to an end at Mill End with the junction with the A4155. **Turn R** and very soon **turn L** to join a public footpath between two cottages after the Hambleden Boat Yard. Walk along this footpath which will take you over a weir system and a lock across the

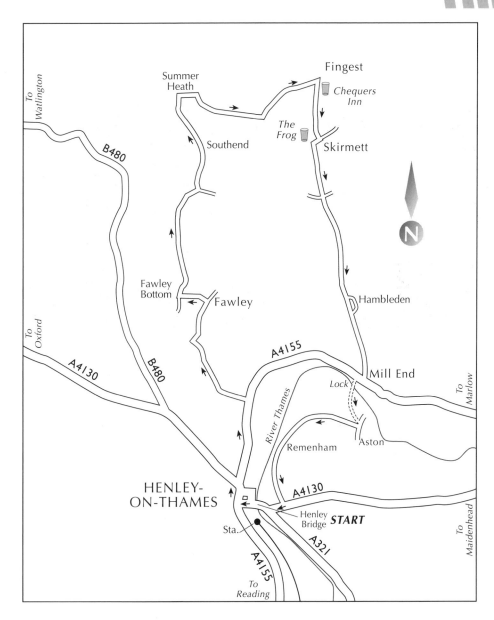

Thames. From the lock **turn L** (footpath sign to Hurley) and join a gravel track. At the fork **bear L** then at the end of the track **turn R** (no signpost) to head for Remenham.

Follow the road through Remenham and on to the T-junction with the A4130 and **turn R**. This will bring you back to the bridge where you started the ride.

The Old Mill, Mill End

HENLEY

The town of Henley is best known for its regatta held in the first week in July since 1839. The races are held between Temple Island and the 18th century bridge in the centre of town. If you would like to find out more about the regatta and also the Thames and its influence on the history, commerce and culture of the places it passes through you can visit the newly opened River and Rowing Museum on Mill Meadows. However, Henley is more than just a town with a regatta. It is set out following a medieval town design and contains many fine buildings including the Victorian Brewery, the 14th century timbered Chantry House and the Kenton Theatre.

HAMBLEDEN

Hambleden is situated at the bottom of a dry valley and is one of the most beautiful villages in the area. The church dates from the 12th century, and there is a still functioning cast iron pump in the centre of the village.

19

Marlow, Lane End and Turville

24½ miles

This circuit starts and ends in the riverside town of Marlow and explores the valleys (or bottoms as they are locally known) to the north, visiting the attractive flint and brick village of Turville en route. This is a ride which looks different in every season.

Map: OS Landranger 175 Reading and Windsor (a small section – around Stokenchurch – is on 165 Aylesbury and Leighton Buzzard but you could manage without it) (GR 851861).

Starting point: This ride starts from the picturesque Regency bridge spanning the Thames in Marlow some 5 miles north of Maidenhead. Marlow may be reached by train from Maidenhead. If arriving by car, there is parking in two car parks either side of the main street. Both are well signed.

There are plenty of possibilities for refreshment in Marlow itself. There are also plenty of pubs around the route. We recommend the Old Sun in Lane End and the Fleur-de-lis in Stokenchurch (on the green). There is plenty of woodland suitable for picnics in the summer, for example Davenport Wood just before the return to Marlow.

The route takes a delightful series of narrow and leafy lanes which link the valleys. Don't be afraid to walk if the gradient gets steep, you are bound to see something interesting. Take care to look out for potholes and loose gravel when descending hills.

Starting from the bridge over the River Thames head into town (north) Go straight on at both mini roundabouts. **Turn L** at the roundabout with the monument (signed A4155, Henley). **Turn R** (signed car park and Bovingdon Green/Frieth). Ride for about 3 miles.

At the crossroads **turn R** (signed Lane End). In Lane End **turn L** at the T-junction (signed Cadmore End). Stay on this road and ride through the edge of Cadmore End (Marlow Road).

Ride into Stokenchurch and **turn L** to join the A40 (signed Oxford).

Marlow suspension bridge

Keep straight on through the village. **Bear L** (signed Ibstone) crossing over the M40 at the Stokenchurch interchange. In Ibstone **turn R** almost immediately after passing a school on the left (single track road, no signpost). Soon there is a sharp left turn followed by a steep descent with a right hand twist (care!). At the T-junction **turn L** (signed Turville). Ride through Turville and then after the village sign **turn R** onto a single track road with a cycle route sign (Watery Lane).

At the T-junction **turn R** and ride into Skirmett. **Turn L** (signed Frieth, single track road) in Skirmett on a right hand bend. At the edge of Frieth **turn R** (signed Henley).

After about 1¼ miles, at Rockwell End, **bear left** at the fork (there is a farm building with a Victorian letter box set in the wall on the right hand side; sign for the right turn reads 'Pheasants Hill'). **Bear L** at the fork (no signpost), soon passing a farm shop on the left. **Turn R** at the T-junction (no signpost). Very soon after a crossroads with farm tracks **turn L** (sign for Henley straight on, and the back of a small cycle sign points into the turning). Shortly you will ride through Bockmer End; keep straight on (signed Marlow).

Soon there is a descent into a valley and an ascent out of it. The sides of the valley are quite steep so care will be needed. You may have to get off and walk if the inclines are too great

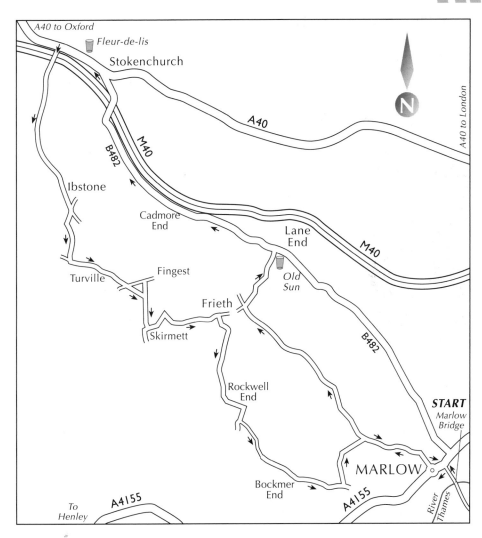

for you. The climb out of the valley is in very picturesque woodland so take time to enjoy it!

At the top of the climb **turn L** (signed Marlow Common) and ride through Davenport Wood. **Turn R** at the T-junction (signed Marlow). **Turn R** at the next T-junction (signed Marlow). Follow the ride through the edge of Marlow to the T-junction with the A4155 and **turn L**. Very soon **turn R** at the roundabout (signed Bisham) to take you back to Marlow Bridge.

MARLOW

This pleasant Thameside town is rich in Georgian architecture which is best appreciated on foot. The suspension bridge which spans the Thames so elegantly was built between 1831 and 1836 as a small scale prototype for the bridge later built over the Danube to connect Buda with Pest in Hungary. From Marlow's bridge, you can stand and watch the water foaming over Marlow weir or the view across to the Compleat Angler inn.

TURVILLE

Turville is a picturesque Chiltern flint and brick village founded, like so many others, in the first half of the 13th century, although the present church mainly dates from the 14th century. The medieval village pub, the Bull and Butcher, is known for its good food, and the restored (and privately owned) windmill perched on a hill overlooking the village provides a well-known local landmark.

20

Egypt, but where are the Pyramids?

19 miles or 23 miles

This ride starts by climbing out of Bourne End (near Maidenhead) and soon passes the entrance to the Cliveden estate whose magnificent house and gardens are owned by the National Trust. It then winds its way to Taplow before turning to take a meandering course which includes Dorney Wood and Burnham Beeches and the village of Egypt. At this point the route makes a northerly 4 mile loop into the pleasant village of Hedgerley. This loop may be cut out, but at the cost of a short stretch of main road. You then return to Bourne End through some pleasantly quiet countryside.

The route may be ridden at any time of year, but it is particularly spectacular in spring when you will be surprised by how many different shades of green there are, and in autumn when the golden beeches and more open views will delight you.

Map: OS Landranger 175 Reading and Windsor (GR 895872).

Starting point: This ride starts from the railway station at Bourne End. The station is served by Thames Trains (bicycles are carried free) and is on the line from Maidenhead. Bourne End is some 4 miles north of Maidenhead and 6 miles north-west of Slough. There is a pay and display car park (free on Sundays, otherwise an hourly rate) which is located off the main A4155 (on Wakeman Lane) and is well signed. From this car park, the railway station is reached by turning left out onto the A4155 and right at the nearby roundabout.

Refreshments are available at Cliveden (NT). There is usually a kiosk on Lord Mayor's Drive, near the Burnham Beeches car park, and there are pubs serving food on the route, for example the Yew Tree (Farnham Common) and the White Horse (Hedgerley).

The route is undulating, with one or two more challenging climbs, for example the initial climb out of Bourne End. The views down towards the river are spectacular, so take your time and enjoy them.

Turn R out of the railway station onto the A4155. About ½ mile from the railway station **turn L** (signed Hedsor/Taplow). At the T-junction **turn R** (signed Taplow, Hedsor Hill). At the end of Bourne End Road **turn**

Navigation by committee!

R at the T-junction (signed Taplow, Cliveden Road).

Soon there is a pub on the left and the entrance to Cliveden on the right. **Bear R** (staying on the 'main road') at the fork (signed Maidenhead, Cliveden Road). **Bear R** at the fork (signed Maidenhead). Close to the junction there is a National Trust car park for the Cliveden Woodlands on the right. Soon after entering Taplow village you will pass Taplow Court on your right. Almost immediately **turn L** (Rectory Road). At the T-junction **turn L** (Hill Farm Road).

At the crossroads **turn R** into Hitcham Lane. At the crossroads turn **L** (no signpost, Taplow Common Road). At the fourth junction on the right **turn R** into Nashdom Lane. Just after passing Nashdom Abbey on the right **turn L** to stay on Nashdom Lane. At the T-junction **turn R** (no signpost). **Turn sharp L** into Dorney Wood Road (signed Dorney Wood). Shortly after Dorney Wood **turn R** (signed Farnham, Curriers Lane). Go straight on at the crossroads; Pumpkin Hill becomes Hawthorn Lane.

Pumpkin Hill and Hawthorn Lane skirt around Burnham Beeches. **Turn L** into the woodlands on the tarmac road signed 'Lord Mayor's Drive' (please note cycling is only

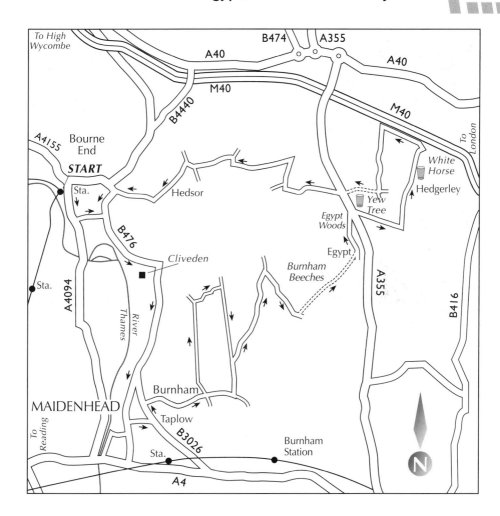

allowed on the tarmac roads within Burnham Beeches). This roadway through Burnham Beeches leads to the main car park at the other side. On leaving the car park **turn L**. Follow the narrow lane between Burnham Beeches and the village of Egypt – Egypt Lane.

If you wish to take the short cut at this point, **turn L** onto the A355 for about ¼ mile and **turn L** into

Harehatch Lane. Otherwise at the A355 **turn L** then immediately **turn R** (signed Hedgerley/Stoke Poges). Go straight on at the crossroads (Hollybush Corner). At the crossroads **turn L** (signed Hedgerley). Keep straight on through the village, joining Village Lane, then **turn L** into Hedgerley Lane. After riding parallel with the M40 to your right for a short distance **turn L** (no signpost or

A ride in springtime

street name). Soon after passing Mount Pleasant Farm, **turn R** at the crossroads to pass Pennlands Farm; this track is classed as a bridle path, but has a good surface. Go straight on at the crossroads with the A355 to join Harehatch Lane.

At the T-junction **turn R** (no signpost) then at the next junction **turn R** (signed Beaconsfield, Ship Hill). Soon after passing Jennings Farm **turn L** – this road is easy to miss! Just after a triangular junction warning sign the road descends sharply with steep banks on either side. On the right hand side of the road there is a green footpath sign pointing to the right. The sign is almost exactly opposite the left hand turn you should take (the road is very narrow). **Turn R** with Castleman's Farm on the right hand corner. **Turn L** at the T-junction (no signpost). **Bear L** (signed Wooburn Common) by staying on the 'main road'. Go straight on (signed Hedsor/Bourne End).

Go straight on at the crossroads then **bear L** on a right hand bend (signed Unsuitable for Motors) passing Hedsor Farm House on the left. At the next junction **turn L** (no signpost). At the crossroads go straight on (the narrow road on the other side is angled to the left and descends steeply) then **turn R** at the T-junction (no signpost). At the T-junction with the A4155 **turn R** to return to the railway station on the left.

CLIVEDEN

The present mansion, built in 1851 in the

classical style by Sir Charles Barry, is the third house to be constructed on the flat hilltop overlooking the River Thames, between Maidenhead and Bourne End. It was built for the Duke of Sutherland. Later it was owned by the Astor family whose entertaining at the house after the First World War made it famous. It is now owned by the National Trust and its extensive grounds with spectacular views down to the river, a water garden, parterre and many miles of woodland paths are open to the public from the beginning of March to the end of December. The mansion itself is used as a prestigious hotel, but a few rooms may be visited on Sundays from April through to October. There is also a woodland car park which is open all year.

BURNHAM BEECHES
Burnham Beeches is an extensive area of ancient woodland and heathland which is owned and managed by the City of London Corporation. It contains a fine collection of pollarded oak and beech trees, many of which are several hundred years old. Please note that cycling is permitted only on the tarmac roads and not on the paths.

FURTHER INFORMATION ABOUT CYCLING IN THE THAMES VALLEY

The Cyclists' Touring Club is the national organisation which represents and campaigns for the interests of all cyclists, whether they ride to work or ride around the world. The club has touring and technical departments to help with all your cycling queries, and issues a bi-monthly magazine to all its members. In the Thames Valley area there are also local CTC groups which organise a variety of led day and half-day rides. All these groups welcome new riders. Rides are led by experienced local cyclists on quiet country roads. If you have enjoyed the rides in this book, why not make contact with your local group and enjoy riding with like-minded people? A list of contact telephone numbers in the region covered by this book are given below. Alternatively there are local groups all over the country, so if you are not local, why not contact the CTC direct to find about groups in your area?

Finally we would both like to thank all our friends in the Oxfordshire CTC, not only for their help checking the routes in this book and their polite enquiries about its progress, but also for their unfailing friendship over the years and for all the expertise and confidence that we have picked up through riding with them.

CTC OXFORDSHIRE DISTRICT ASSOCIATION
Oxford: (01865 461035)
Witney: (01993 705660)
Wantage: (01488 72177)

Email: Oxfordctc@aol.com
Website:
http://members.aol.com/oxfordctc

CTC READING DISTRICT ASSOCIATION
(01344 420031)
Website: www.i-way.co.uk/reading-ctc

CTC SOUTH BUCKS DISTRICT ASSOCIATION
(01296 696229)
Email: 106462.643@compuserve.com

CTC (CYCLISTS' TOURING CLUB) NATIONAL HEADQUARTERS
Telephone (Help Desk): 01483 417217
Email: Cycling@ctc.org.uk
Website: www.ctc.org.uk